NOT OUT

CW00428378

E

Jared E. Collins

To Rob,

With very best wishes

from

Peter Adams,

aka Jared E. Collins

Published by

COLLINS
AMBERLEY   NORTHAM   DEVON

British Library Cataloguing-in-Publication Data.
A catalogue record for this book is available
from the British Library.

Arthur H. Stockwell Ltd., bear no responsibility
for the accuracy of events recorded in this book.

The net proceeds from the sale of this book
will be donated to Bideford Cricket Club.

ISBN 0-9546119-0-X
Printed in Great Britain by
Arthur H. Stockwell Ltd.
Torrs Park   Ilfracombe
Devon

Not Out — Impossible

It is difficult to remember exactly where it all started but perhaps it was with a discussion on Christmas presents. The season almost appears to be getting out of hand with costly cards, postage and the subliminal effect of television where it is no longer a question of a basic present but the request is for designer gear, whatever the extent of interest in a particular sport or pastime. Trainer shoes at almost £100 for a teenager with the minimal of aspirations to achieve, or yet £900 for a mountain bike.

What were your best presents as a child? I remember two things. Intense negotiations with a reluctant parent to allow me to draw out £3.10s from my Post Office Savings Account to purchase a second-hand bicycle after giving an undertaking to clean it every day, and the purchase of well-used football boots from a master at school who collected school items from those about to leave. These amounted to clothing and other items, which, if purchased new, would have used up limited clothing coupons for items which were no longer of use to those wishing to launch themselves into an unsuspecting world.

The boots trod many a mile in the local park and the bicycle, modest by present day standards with only one gear, no headlight and a painful saddle, took me into the great unknown with regular visits to the seaside and inland to grace playing fields with ninety minutes of unbridled endeavour and often muddy encounter.

It was an easy little ride down to the park where all sports were played on the same oval of grass around which there was a cycle track. As with so many things, the cycle track became abused with 'time trials' and racing became the order of the day with or without a roller skater clinging frantically to the rear of the saddle. Grazed knees were commonplace which was not helped by the fact that short trousers were worn until one reached the dramatic age of fifteen (or more).

No one ever marked out a proper cricket pitch but two coats would do as wickets, hopefully someone would turn up with something resembling a bat, and a tennis ball would do unless someone had managed to 'acquire' a baseball from one of the many American servicemen billeted at Instow during the war. Somewhat hard, not entirely round, this type of ball was much more of a challenge than the softer tennis ball variety and much more manly, making us into hardened sportsmen.

The worst thing about such encounters was the way in which those with the equipment would automatically become captains and the remainder would have to line up so the captains could select their team by taking turns in picking out the best, and how embarrassing it was to be the last and regarded as completely useless. The games never seemed to reach a satisfactory conclusion as the owner of the bat was never out. It was virtually impossible to hit the crumpled coat serving as the wicket as it only stood a few inches above the ground. LBWs were never in front, and, in any event, there was no umpire. Catches were rarely held, particularly if we were playing with a hard ball.

It was much the same at school. We did have a groundsman but his main requirement was that necessary to cultivate the vegetable patch which supplied produce to the school kitchens, and this was a much more rewarding exercise than endless hours of cutting and rolling wickets. In any event the pitch had a fair slope towards the lower boundary, and no amount of rolling would produce perfection upon which the budding Comptons of that era could blossom.

Sports afternoon took the form of two captains being chosen by the master in charge. The 'Park Method' of team selection followed, and after the most promising twenty-two had been chosen, the rabble was dismissed to the upper field on an even greater slope to while away the hour whilst the select had the luxury of wickets, a few grubby pads and brown "Les Ames" bats. The ball had at one time had a seam which was battered into the surrounding leather. The stitching more often than not was defective so that a whitish tuft of hair emerged from the split seam which provided adhesion for the spinner, enlarged the size of the ball and made it quite difficult to hit very far. The boundary fences accommodated the deficiency rather well, all being relatively close to the wicket.

At the highest level, the cricketing world was just opening up with Compton and Edrich performing miracles at Lords. This was the age of Brylcreem, county caps similar to those we wore to school, batting gloves with green rubber spikes sewn onto the thumb and each finger, and pads stout with protective bamboo and horsehair. Marketing was just beginning to enter the scene and autographed bats were attracting the signatures of new heroes, our heroes whom we might be fortunate to see in the flesh but as yet not on TV. These heroes had a godly talent, once seen never to be forgotten.

I digress. Fourteen was a difficult age. I was not always the last to be selected from that attentive line of young hopefuls awaiting selection in the park and I felt I had achieved some kind of goal when I was selected for the School Colts XI, the under fifteens. I quickly acquired a second-hand pair of white flannels from the art teacher (now in charge of the second-hand store). Boots were more difficult to obtain so my gymshoes would have to do, and I did have an Airtex shirt which would complete my ensemble. Less than a week before my debut, I developed a verruca on the bottom of my foot, contracted at the local swimming pool, and an extraction followed by a stitch deprived the school of its No.11 batsman and fifth change bowler.

I was reflecting the other day how different school life was. Firstly, most of us walked to the school from wherever. For those living at Appledore (a mere three miles), they caught the service bus but still had a mile to walk from the bus terminus to the school. Torrington was seven miles by rail, then the mile, whereas Ernie Stoneman, who lived at Middle Gribble, an outer lesser known hamlet to the south of Great Torrington, cycled three miles to Torrington Station before the seven mile rail trip and at least a further mile on foot to the hall of educational excellence. I lived about a mile away, but had to walk mostly up hill in the early morning. The school bell went at 12.20 p.m. for the lunch break — we walked the mile home, ate a meal, and embarked on the second mile to be back for the 1.40 p.m. call to classes. Four miles a day, twenty miles a week and this began at ten years and went on until sixteen — no wonder our legs were pretty sturdy. Oh! one other thing — I wore short trousers (as did most) until I was fifteen revealing muscular, strong and occasionally sunburnt legs — quite a start to an inauspicious sporting career.

I don't know why, but I became a little troubled by my upper body strength which was not developing at the same speed as my legs. Weight was another problem and I remember being quite anxious to achieve something beyond nine and a half stones without having to wear my Army Cadet boots! At that time, one hardly ever opened a newspaper without seeing an advert featuring Charles Atlas — "Mr Universe". He had a body like no other and attributed his extraordinary build and development to the use of chest expanders which he was pleased to sell to any weakling at a modest cost.

I was most impressed and invested wisely in this elementary device which consisted of two attractive handles with four coiled springs connecting the two. Fortunately, the springs were detachable and I found it impossible to pull the expanders at all with four

"He had a body like no other . . ."

springs attached, whereupon one of the springs was quickly removed, allowing much greater versatility. It was, however, still something of a feat to fully extend the three springs throughout the whole of the prescribed exercises. The chest expander could be held directly in front of the body and the arms fully extended to the side; a foot could be inserted in one end and the other extended by the bent arm thus causing pain to the biceps, then there was the extension with the springs behind the head. The latter could be very painful if the arms became tired and the springs retracted rather quickly, trapping the hairs at the back of the neck. This usually happened at the end of the exercise, when one became tired, and it was not easy to release the hair which, more often than not, had to be sacrificed — a very painful experience.

I found the most difficult to be the "hands over the head" technique where the arms then had to be pulled down to the horizontal — really testing the springs. With such intimate exercises, I invariably carried them out in the privacy of my small (very small) bedroom at the top of the stairs. It was a very cold room (we had no central heating nor other form of heating) and it was healthy (so my mother said) to keep the window open at all times. There was just about room to stand between my single bed and the chest of drawers, and that was it. The ceiling was somewhat low, with a central light hanging from the ceiling.

What I did not take into account was the lampshade! I tried the difficult manoeuvre at the end of a sequence — arms extended upwards, stretching the springs to the full by extending the arms to the side, and, on the return journey, I felt that all my strength had gone (it had been a long and vigorous session) and the springs snapped together rather rapidly trapping the fringe of the lampshade. I simply did not have the strength to once more extend the springs and the chest expanders remained hanging from the lampshade for three or four days until I had built up my strength and confidence once again. I often wondered if Charles Atlas had ever encountered this problem!

My summer holidays were invariably spent with an aunt (my favourite aunt) at Taunton, the home of Somerset County Cricket. Many are the days when I would go along to the pre-season nets to watch the professionals warm up and coach the sons of members. To be close to these extraordinary men who could do so much with bat and ball and at the same time be so entertaining was a real thrill. The Taunton ground was magic with its small boundaries, churches nearby singing out their hourly (and sometimes quarterly) chimes, and the River Tone where Arthur Wellard regularly dispatched cricket balls. The pavilion was a splendid Victorian monstrosity, mostly of wooden construction liberally covered with green and cream paint, and with the smallest of scoreboxes attached.

I well remember the first time I saw a touring side play at Taunton. It was the Indian team in 1946 and this game had a lasting effect on me. The visitors batted first and Bill Andrews, a rangy quick bowler, charged in from one end whilst that economic master of swing, Bertie Buse, calmly walked the first four or so paces of his run up, followed by a gentle four more strides before a whippy action sent the ball in a wavering arc towards the attentive batsman. The innings was all over before lunch with only sixty-four runs on the board — we had seen complete mastery of the ball over bat.

I subsequently bought a second-hand ball from Bill Andrews (was it the one which had consistently found its way through the Indian defences?) and could say with pride that I had spoken to the great man (it was to ask the price and say thank you afterwards) but this armed me for further escapades in the park at home where I could now dictate terms as ball owner.

Somerset seemed to bat on a different wicket and scored consistently. I saw another of the Gods of Cricket, Harold Gimblett, who, with the greatest of ease, could lift a slightly overpitched ball into the nearby churchyard whether it was the first ball of the innings or the last. The quality of the bowling mattered, not the time of day.

The Indians had their stars and I remember Lala Amarnath who eased up to the wicket and departed a certain amount of zip on the ball by bringing his arm over rather quickly, twice in succession, before releasing the ball. Later in my career, the double arm swinger was introduced into my repertoire in the hope that the batsman would play a shot the first time around and not be composed by the time the second arc was completed and the ball released.

I was amazed to subsequently read a book about Harold Gimblett concerning his professional career which started in the 1930s when Somerset had no coach, only six professionals, and regularly made up the side with local cricketers or chaps down from the universities. Harold himself was obliged to seek advice from cricketers with other counties on how to play the specialist bowlers and, more to the point, this advice was freely given. Cricket was played in a certain spirit which unfortunately is rarely found in today's arena.

The cricketers were all shapes and sizes which added colour to the game. We all heard tales about Denis Compton turning up at the wrong grounds, arriving resplendent in dinner jacket from the night before and then turning in a vintage performance of superlative stroke play. At the other end of the scale we had Somerset's own Horace Hazell. I am sure he would have been the first to admit that his rotund shape would not have labelled him a professional sportsman and his ability with the bat made it necessary for him to retain the No.11 spot, but his complete control and flight as a left-handed spin bowler ensured that when Horace was bowling, the batsmen had to work for their runs, attack his bowling, which inevitably resulted in good cricket all round.

Probably by this time, the seed had been sown. This was a game to be enjoyed, it tolerated the characters, it was often played in sunshine and we had our heroes to follow. Perhaps I am trying to make a comparison between then and now — how good were we and is it the same game we played then. I have no doubt it was a different game for many, many reasons.

A 1952 Cricket Year Book for the South West suggests that there were cricket leagues in the Plymouth and Exeter areas but elsewhere there were only friendlies (not all that friendly!) and knock out competitions. My club Bideford had had a good season that year, playing fifty-two games, winning thirty-two, losing thirteeen, drawing six and one was abandoned because of rain. The best batting average was about thirty, the best bowler getting a wicket for every eight runs scored. One other North Devon Club I espied suggested that the batting had been a great improvement on the previous year, showing an average of over nine! Yes, it was a different game.

Another major difference was the opportunities offered to the younger players. After school cricket, there were no colts teams and it was rather a case that if you were good enough you were big enough. Coaching for the ordinary club player was unheard of and it was very much a case of starting at the bottom and working your way upwards. This particularly applied to myself batting at No.11 and being fifth change bowler. Fortunately I did enjoy fielding but without a 2nd team or colts XI, it was a case of 1st team or nothing — not ideal if you were expecting a game a week. Hence I often diverted into tennis and swimming and sometimes two or three sports did not mix and the wrong limbs became tired. There were exceptions to the rule and for the most part these were boys and young men who had been fortunate enough to go to private schools where coaching was provided accompanied by regular practice.

1948 — The changeover year, the year when we took our School Certificate Examinations which obviously took priority over sporting activities but in between times we were looking for some relaxation. One of my friends had acquired a Denis Compton bat and would allow anyone to bowl at him for hours on end and he found me a willing ally. It was no good bowling the same thing all the time, so some deliveries were off a short run, some a much longer approach, some over the wicket, some around, and this seemed to go on for days at an end. He certainly got better with the bat — I simply became more tired! The school that year, however, had a good side, well balanced including a few good all-rounders and we did play against some senior sides.

The ground at Westward Ho! was subsequently to be my home ground for many, many years. I first played there in June 1948 not realising the historic associations of this famous strip of green. Further inland is what is now "Kipling Terrace", a mass of modern flats, but originally it was The United Services College, of Rudyard Kipling fame. Presumably at the time he was at the college, the grounds swept down to the sea, with the lower section being the cricket ground and, beyond it, the pebble ridge and the sea. This continues to be the case and whenever I step out onto the playing area looking upwards, I see the old college looking down and feel how lucky I am to have played for so many years in such beautiful surroundings with the glorious Atlantic surging in the background, a mere big hit away.

Captain of the Bideford club round about that time was Dick Swain, one of many who gave so much time to local cricket in the area, and he was known as "3 over Dick". This related to his tactical masterplan — give everyone three overs with the ball, and there shouldn't be many complaints.

I had forgotten my first ever game at Westward Ho! which was against C.O.X.E. During the Second World War, the Combined Operations Experimental Engineers had a camp in the village from which the soldiers carried out experiments with amphibious warfare. Vehicles would be waterproofed and taken across the burrows and out to sea where they either sank or floated off into the surf, hopefully to return. C.O.X.E. shared the ground with Bideford and it was in June 1948, that the local grammar school was invited to play at Westward Ho! — for me it was the very first time. The wicket must have suited, as I came away with five wickets.

The second visit, a week or so later, had much greater significance. It was against the Bideford Wednesday XI (mostly shopkeepers) and this proved a much sterner test. For me it was a meeting with one of the finest and nicest sportsmen to come from these parts, Peter Trapnell, a gentleman in every respect. Peter captained the Bideford side against us and immediately took pity on us with but one bag of gear for the whole team. The contents were somewhat sparse — three Les Ames bats, three pairs of horsehair pads, three pairs of gloves with green rubber lumps and that was about it. The pavilion in those days was a rather small wooden hut with slatted seats and a central table. It was certainly difficult for all eleven to change together. Wooden floors and seats resulted in one of the major injuries being from "splinters", which if acquired from a seat usually meant that you quickly found out who your true friends were.

Bideford decided to bat and we prepared for some leather chasing in the field. Our keeper was a rather diminutive Peter Loughlin who, just as he was going out through the door and down the two steps onto the pitch, was asked by home captain Peter Trapnell "Would you like a box?" Peter, in his innocence, replied "I can see alright over the stumps without one, thank you."

In August I was asked to play for Bideford at home and the final game was Ilfracombe away when several lessons were learnt. After taking the first wicket at nought, the second fell at one hundred and forty-eight — yes, club cricketers did score hundreds in those days (this one had a jazz hat — I remember it well). The local newspaper recalled that *Collins bowled slow spinners in his second spell taking four wickets, and Ilfracombe were all out for 158.* This was the match when I was first introduced to that well known species, the bald vicar bowling lofted leg-breaks. Most sides seemed to have had one at that time, and they all encouraged the

"Would you like a box?"

most dainty footwork, usually accompanied by a charge, with little thought for actually striking the ball. The season had been a learning curve.

1949— I started where I had left off but with five wickets against Bude *"after reverting to spinners"*. All this charging up to the wicket doesn't seem to make much sense, but if you bowl slow, how can you get mad! Being available for most of the season, I perhaps expected great things, but unless one had a very good pedigree, it was a case of batting at No.11 and being fifth change bowler, until an opportunity arose to disprove the captain's assessment.

Our fixture list at Westward Ho! followed a decided pattern. For the most part, we played away in May and the rest of the season we were at home to local teams and touring sides. Being on the coast, Westward Ho! was always an attraction in addition to which, a general lack of transport made the cricket ground a very popular venue over the weekend, particularly when the tide was in. Some of our visitors were of a very high standard and it was therefore essential for us to improve to be able to compete and provide a contest commensurate with our splendid location.

Our away fixtures were always a joy as it gave us an opportunity of seeing how the others lived. In June 1949, I well remember my first visit to Bishops Tawton. The ground, as far as I remember, was down a track, beneath a railway bridge and the small but level ground was bounded on two sides by a bow in the River Taw, and the railway track was just beyond the third boundary.

We arrived about thirty minutes prior to the start and the pitch was fenced off with a number of wooden poles supporting barbed wire intended to keep larger animals off the actual playing area. Removal of the fencing involved a player taking each post and walking off in orderly fashion. This manoeuvre was carried out with military precision but nothing was done to cover the six or so deep holes. Also beyond the cut area, the surround was of tufted grass liberally decorated with cow pats — a fielder's nightmare. A fishing net was provided to retrieve balls from the river.

The changing accommodation was a hut on stilts. It must have had nine or more steps leading up to the wooden structure on high, well above any anticipated flood level when the river was in full spate. As far as I remember, the two teams shared the hut without division and there was a well positioned club notice board bearing averages, indicating that "Butcher" Slee was having another glorious season with a bowling average of just under two, closely followed by "Whacker" Nutt who was struggling to keep his bowling average under three. "Butcher" was, in fact, a very good swiftish left-handed bowler who had done greater things in the prewar era and had a "sun-blind" blazer to prove it.

Our first wicket stand was monumental, totalling fifty-nine runs and the newspaper report suggested it *"would have been worth more on a well-cut outfield"*. My recollection is that all fifty-nine were in singles, the ball racing off the limited square only to halt virtually immediately once in the long grass. The batters were not skilful enough to aim for the holes left by the removed poles holding up the barbed wire but I think I recall one of their chaps running three when one of our fielders with a shorter arm than most failed to retrieve the ball accurately placed by a Bishops Tawton veteran who knew every inch of the ground including the exact position of the pole holes. Short balls bowled by visitors were dispatched without ceremony either onto the railway line to be retrieved with a chipping or two embedded, or the river when bowling with a wet ball did nothing for morale.

I am not really sure how we managed to net practice. Some sections of netting were erected anywhere, a light roller was applied and away we went. Something like a dozen new cricket balls were used during a season, to be taken home, scrubbed and polished in time for the next game. Being a change bowler, I cannot ever remember the luxury of seeing the maker's name in

*". . . one of our fielders with a
shorter arm than most . . ."*

gold on the side of the ball — it had been long extinguished before I was handed the red missile. In any case, new balls were not good for the fingers which in those days would rip the fingers to bits, necessitating a lengthy recovery by way of the main digit being soaked very regularly in methylated spirit. This proved somewhat of a folly in that instead of the finger blistering, it simply split which was much more painful. If only I had been able to read Richie Benaud's book written many years later, at the end of which he explained in great detail his remedy for overcoming this dreaded spinner's lurgy.

At one of these nets I batted against a newcomer, Robbie, a giant of a man from Yorkshire, who spoke in a strange tongue and brought with him strange habits. His first ball hit the top of the net and I was not impressed, but he turned out to be a superb cricketer, a great reader of the game, able to place the ball on any spot, and make the batsman play the shot that he (Robbie) wanted him to play. Many times I have seen him make one change in the field and the batsman would hit the next ball to that fielder. The bat looked small in his massive hands and he was not a great believer in running between wickets but preferred rattling the boundary or even better still, clearing it. The lusty blow was usually followed by the most delicate of late cuts — it was pure magic. His approach to the wicket when batting was unique. It was always accompanied by a tuneless whistle. His first act upon reaching the wicket was to measure, with bat and handle, the distance between the two creases, and he would stand his bat upright and then take guard. He never did trust the groundsman, or whoever marked out the pitch, and his tuneless whistle obviously disoriented the bowler on many an occasion having regard to the ease with which Robbie subsequently scored runs.

It was in September that we had a visit from John Tanous XI. This was a touring side with some very good professionals and my first experience of playing against first-class cricketers. I well remember Don Taylor, a New Zealand opening bat who also played for Warwickshire, coming to the wicket. I fancied my chances at cover point but when he hit the ball towards me I seriously wondered if it might be the more sensible option to get out of the way and let the ball go for four. It was cricket in a different dimension. E. Watts from Surrey also played, and young Mr Collins, batting up a bit at No.6 and hoping to make an impression, stepped back to the first ball from a county spinner to hit his own wicket before the ball arrived! This was not the way to impress.

1950 — I realise now how immature we were as club cricketers. Many around me were natural sportsmen whose abilities changed from the large inflated ball to the small solid one as soon as April came to an end, and balance, good eyesight and a competitive nature took over. Some players were very good but for the most part, when the first four or five were knocked over, most of the resistance had gone. Wickets were not as good so team scores were usually get-at-able with a fair wind.

And so 1950 came and went. As a player I did not improve, though occasionally I was allowed to bat a little higher up the order, and fifth change, sometimes became third, but I was not guaranteed a permanent place in an improving 1st XI with no 2nd XI to fall back on and develop skills.

I believe I did purchase a new pair of cricket boots — when I say "new", they were boots to replace my plimsolls which did not smell too good after a few years' toil but which at the same time were so easy to carry in my brown paper carrier bag with *"A. R. L. Adams, Family Grocer"* emblazoned on one side. This might have been regarded as the forerunner of sponsorship — the bag went everywhere with me.

The boots, perhaps, deserve a special mention. My front foot always came down with a bit of a thump, despite a tendency towards a four pace run up, but a leaning towards weak ankles suggested that a sturdy boot might help. Thinking back, the boots were quite unbelievable having white canvas uppers, leather soles with sturdy heal and little metal studs which had to be firmly driven in with a hammer after wetting the sole first to afford easier access to the studs. Invariably some went in at an angle and lasted but a short while but it didn't seem to matter as the boots invariably gave up the ghost after no more than one year when the canvas simply disintegrated with continual wear and the sweaty nature of the occupants.

I forgot to say that a favourite of the Westward Ho! players was the splendid bedsocks sold at Trapnell's the drapers (it was sense to support our captain, he might remember this when called upon to make a tense decision to change the bowling).

Edging a ball into my lower abdomen at the age of sixteen against Braunton persuaded me that a jockstrap and box might be a useful investment. Having made enquiries, I was pointed in the direction of the sports outfitters in the main street, a largish shop (by our standards), one half of which was a toy shop. It had a relatively small staff and as I required a rather personal accoutrement, I endeavoured to single out the gentleman assistant who happened to be in the toy department, but I was waylaid by the rather young and attractive lady assistant who politely asked if she could be of assistance. I thought she might, but not on my present mission, and I looked sheepishly at the boxed jockstraps secreted behind the counter. She noticed my glance and asked (in what I felt at the time was a seductive tone) "What size?" I now had to think very quickly on my feet. I was not sure in my own mind, how such things were measured. If I blurted out twenty-eight inches, she might have fainted on the spot, on the other hand, a single figure measurement could have been the disclosure of a very vital piece of information to a complete stranger. I chose the former and chose well. I was not invited to try on my purchase and left the shop well satisfied that I had acted with honour and not without a fair amount of guile.

"What size?"

The season came and went — I remember it brought about a first visit to Filleigh where I was introduced to Bob McRae's wobblers. We met many strange bowlers during our travels and Bob's windmill action which followed a brisk walk to the wicket resulted in the ball swinging one way and then the other during the initial period of its flight. This was very taxing on the mind particularly as the ball took quite a while to arrive by which time the batsman's mind was in complete turmoil. One suspects that Bob had already worked this out but was not prepared to pass the finer points of his methodology on to lesser mortals. Such is the way with all great bowlers, some ideas, but not all, are shared.

A yardstick in those days was the North Devon Cricket Club whose splendid venue was the beautiful cricket ground alongside the Taw Estuary at Instow, with Appledore and the confluence of the two rivers, the Taw and the Torridge, forming the background. Coupled with the fact that the pavilion is thatched (and also the score hut), fronting onto a splendid swathe of green of county proportions, makes this a ground to savour and where performances are magnified by the magnificence of the surroundings. A write up of that year suggested that there were only three other clubs in the country (at that time) which could boast a longer period of continuous play — *"but none can have a better setting"*.

At this time, the Instow CC used the ground on Saturdays whereas North Devon CC played on Sundays and for the most part entertained the tourists. It really was a question of what's in a name as frequently both sides had the same personnel. It is probably true to say that North Devon CC were never without a county player or two and they certainly have had many excellent players over the years that have been associated with them.

This was where I, as a young man, went to see some real cricket played and marvelled at what could be achieved. As far as spectators were concerned, the shirt was not removed on a hot summer's day — the groundsman immediately came around to require you to dress appropriately or else leave the ground, and the batting orders were displayed at the entrance to the ground. It was not uncommon in those days to take a scorebook with you and keep the score.

My friend and I went along to see one match and he read from the list while I wrote the batting order in my small scorebook. He came to the name "Onions" and pronounced this in the usual culinary way and a rather splendidly dressed gentleman in striped blazer and jazz hat coughed and said "Oh! Ni-yons." No wonder foreigners find our language so difficult!

It is perhaps interesting to note that the Instow top batting average on Saturdays was 24.72 and bowling 7, whereas on Sundays and against touring sides, the North Devon top batter averaged 34.5 and the bowler 7.6.

1951/52 — It is rather difficult to contemplate in today's social climate, that one could be sent a postcard advising that Her Majesty (it was "His" in my day!) required you to attend for a medical prior to National Service, which at that time was a two-year jaunt at a destination at His/Her Majesty's pleasure at a minimal wage, but food and clothing were to be provided.

The medical was an occasion of its own particularly when we remembered the embarrassment of visiting the school nurse for the first time. As well as a lot of poking and prodding, we were measured and I remember stepping away from the vertical ruler, with horizontal pole which rested on the head to indicate the height. As I stepped away from this complicated piece of machinery, I could see the pole sliding down, and my 5'8" quickly became 5'3" immediately guaranteeing the Army victory when my leaving medical (in two years' time) would indicate how much I had grown.

Peter Hawke (otherwise known as 'Awke), a very fine cricketer, learned man, speaker and storyteller extraordinaire, decided that his tactic, as far as the Army was concerned, would be to act the village idiot.

In fairness, his call to arms did not relate to National Service, but rather the real thing some years earlier. Peter recalls how he attended for his medical together with some doubtful character who was adamant that he would not be taking part in any hostilities and that he had a sure-fire way of failing his medical. Peter listened to all this quite intently, the fellow went in to see the doctor and came out all smiles. "How did you get on" enquired Peter.

"M.E. came the reply, medically excused." Peter was most impressed and asked how this avoidance of service was achieved. "I wore a truss" came the matter of a fact reply. "You can have it if you like."

Peter jumped at the thought — this might be the lifeline he was looking for. He duly put on the medical appliance, limped in to see the doctor, and was subjected to a rather demanding inspection at the end of which, the doctor simply said "M.E."

"Medically excused?" enquired Peter.

"No" came the reply "Middle East. Anyone who can wear a truss upside down, can surely ride a camel!"

Peter did end up in Egypt!

1951/52 were years spent in the Royal Artillery, but life for some was much better than for others, and following a series of courses and postings, I came to rest in Nottingham as a clerk in an Army Group of the Royal Artillery (Territorial). This literally meant going into the city each day to work in an office, except when I was seconded to another group for manoeuvres which usually took the form of summer camps, greatly interfering with any prospect of cricket.

I needed a scrapbook to remind me that I played for Lenton 2nds and finished second in the bowling averages which meant absolutely nothing! At some stage I had taken five wickets and a Trevor Redgate took me out for a drink to celebrate. At some stage that evening, after a number of ales, he asked if I played soccer and when I said "Yes", he suggested that he could arrange a game for me. I was due to go home on leave and took my soccer boots back with me. On telephoning Trevor, he questioned as to whether he had in fact offered to get me a game and I began to have serious doubts.

A card duly arrived, inviting me to play for a 3rd XI at Stanton Ironworks the following Saturday. This was fine until Friday afternoon when a hurried phone call asked if I could play in London the following day. I asked my civilian chief clerk, he said "OK" and I was asked to meet some of the team at Nottingham Station early in the morning for the trip to London. I was hastily introduced to a few of the chaps, the rest would be meeting us in the capital city, a destination completely unknown to me. We gathered, went along to a massive recreation ground owned by a national bank, and a sheet on the notice board indicated that our team was about to play the bank 1st XI — one of nine bank teams being fielded that day! We played, won 2-1, everyone else in our team was ecstatic, but I was just whacked having covered most blades of grass from a wing half position.

The previous year, the bank side, Westminster Bank 1st XI, had beaten our team in the semi-final of the A.F.A. Cup, a national competition, and we had turned the tables on them! What I did not realise was that our team and committee had strong connections with county cricketers and members had included Reg Simpson (Notts and England), H. Ramsay Cox (Notts), Guy Willatt (Notts, Derby and Middlesex), Ken Taylor (our captain who opened the batting for Warwicks), Dickie Sale (Warwicks and Derbyshire) and Frank Woodhead (Notts) to name but a few. Ken was a magnificent man, a fine footballer, who ran most games from the centre of the park. His best advice to me as a midfielder was "Never get beaten on the halfway line" — simple but so effective.

I was invited to meet the members for an informal chat and pint in a pub at the back of the central square in Nottingham, and the conversation quickly got around to cricket and Frank Woodhead said that he thought Wally was a better player than Don (having played against both!).

I stupidly said "Wally? Don?"

"Hammond and Bradman" — Frank had played against both in their primes.

I was out of my depth and when asked if I played, I thought it prudent to say "No."

We also had first-hand stories about Denis Compton, and his penchant for turning up at the wrong ground at the wrong time, and when he eventually found the correct destination, he was still able to go out to bat and score runs with alarming ease.

No helmets were worn in those days and there was very little padding — I cannot believe the bowlers were slower than they are today — but the bats were lighter and the ball was there to be hit. There seems to be much more fear in the game today, less pleasure and, perhaps even more disappointing, less sportsmanship — I digress.

1953 — This was perhaps a "sorting out" period — was this the game for me? Would I enjoy it? I had left the Army in March having just had a plaster cast removed from my leg following a tendon injury and certainly soccer was out of the question.

At that time I preferred soccer (and later rugby), as after ninety minutes of serious endeavour, there was a result and I could get involved as much or as little as I wanted, commensurate with trying to keep fit. Once the whistle went, you were in the thick of it, whereas with cricket, the afternoon could be a boring couple of hours fielding in a position not recognised by the batsmen, and it became very easy to daydream. The batting sensation could be over in a flash — one good ball and you were homeward bound, dreaming about what would happen on your next visit to the wicket.

The games were all friendlies, due to start at 2.30 p.m., and winning the toss gave a team the opportunity of batting first for two to two and a half hours, taking tea and restricting the opposition to just over two hours. You could, of course, declare early with powerful batsmen and strike bowlers. Alternatively, if you did not have too good a side, you would put the opposition in, hopefully to bat out a draw in the lesser amount of time allowed after tea. The joy which we derived from this format over the next sixteen years was enormous due to a fine nucleus of cricketers, joined at intervals by top-up men of quality, but the keeping together, the quality of some of the players and the lack of a second or colts team was eventually our undoing. There must be continuity.

A short cv of some of the players would not seem out of place. I have already mentioned Robbie, the Yorkshireman. I think he set us new targets, taught us how to think more about the game, and also that the game was not over until the last ball. He would play anywhere at any time, often to our annoyance, as the same day that he would cry off for a game at Westward Ho!, A. N. Other would be playing elsewhere exactly on the route which Robbie covered as what in those days was designated as a commercial traveller, i.e. a travelling salesman. He was invariably late and did like a drop of ale after the game which sadly was not available at Westward Ho! at that time. Most clubs were lucky to have changing accommodation let alone anything else. He was a mighty man in all respects as some of his later achievements would show.

Our skipper (and probably the best I have ever served under, though there are a few others with a very good case) was Ray Bird. Another giant, over six feet tall and nineteen stones in weight, though, on medical advice, he lost at least four stones in later years. He was an opening bat, very much a touch player, but his reading of a game was second to none. He would take off a bowler to protect him, he would introduce a special type of bowler if the incoming batsman had a weakness. He knew the laws of cricket backwards and always had an able assistant at hand in the person of P. Hawke. One suspected that the opposing batsmen were always under discussion and I well remember the occasion when the opposition was chasing a modest one hundred and twenty runs and were in the eighties for the loss of one wicket. I felt that we were never going to lose that game. We did not. Ray played for the team. On another occasion he declared with a young player on ninety-eight not out — it was in the team's best interest and the player (who counted his runs as he scored them) was well aware when the declaration was to take place and should have got a move on. If we were not scoring fast enough, he got himself out deliberately to make way for a stroke player. If we had a very good side, he often dropped to No.8. The captain doing his best for the team — you could not ask for more.

Another major character was Bill Shortridge. Bill had been through the 1930's depression, out of work and struggling, and to while away the hours he had learnt to play the piano. By the time I got to know him, he must have been forty (this seems very old when you are twenty) and in fairness to Bill, he did spend quite a bit of time with me, telling me what a bowler's length was and even had me bowling at a cigarette packet which he had placed on a length on the practice wicket to try to introduce a bit of control. He had immense confidence in his bowling and his No.1 fan was probably Peter Hawke who nicknamed him "Two-spin Hagen." Bill's stock ball was his flighted leg-spinner which he delivered off about eight paces and if hit, the next ball went even higher. If you fielded in close, you could see the batsman's eyes light up. This was usually followed by a dancing charge and then mayhem in different parts of the ground depending upon whether the batsman hit the ball or missed it. Bill also bowled a sneaky off-break but wondered how the batsmen knew it was coming. It may have been something to do with the fact that he approached the wicket at double the speed with the ball in his right hand, whereas for the legger, the ball was held in the left hand awaiting a late transferral! Bill could always be identified on the field, however near or far, by a thick leather fireman's belt which he always wore around his middle supporting white flannels which were always shorter than most. A great character.

Alan Bidgood was a banker and a useful all-rounder. Mainly an early batter anxious to hit the ball, he was not known for big scores but made many a useful contribution. His fielding was irregular, the brilliant being followed by overthrows and he was known as a "shock" bowler. His run up consisted of a step, an enormous leap into the air following which his arms dragged the ground, and then a charge to the wicket where he could deliver a very quick ball. Not necessarily a stock bowler to keep the batsmen quiet, he was very often the breaker of annoying stands. A good club man.

Rodney Beer was a sportsman par excellence. A young man, he found ball games very easy to play and could have made a success at any number of sports. Whilst at school he played Western League football for the local club, the best available locally, and he had to be told at sixteen that unless he played rugby for the school, his football activities with the local football club would have to cease. Later Rodney was to play for the county at rugby. He became a single figure handicap golfer. A magnificent stroke player, electric fielder and quick bowler, he was always very much involved in any game he played and a born match winner.

Gerry Waldon was captain at the time I first played and he was a very steady opening bowler, not particularly quick, but he was adept at bringing the ball back into the batsman and was never easy to get away. He could also wield a useful bat and was a very solid performer who could be relied upon.

Cliff Cudmore was our keeper, and although he had opened, was probably our lesser member with the bat. This was no bad thing as it meant that we batted all the way down. Cliff was a "stopper" and apart from Bill Shortridge with his telegraphed deliveries, he was not a good "reader" of the bowler.

Without coaching being readily available, I had purchased a splendid book *"How to bowl them out"* by C. B. Fry. This was a truly amazing publication and in deciding that I had some talent as a bowler and wished to become better, I read the book thoroughly and decided to invent one or two routines to give myself a comprehensive repertoire. Fry had referred to the "Spofforth" half ball, where the ball lay halfway in the palm of the hand with the other half protruding.

Keith Miller, who frequented these shores with the Australians, had perfected the "Miller Roundarm". This was a magnificent ball delivered with the fingers down one side of the seam to make the ball shoot off in the opposite direction, but it was delivered with a round arm motion. To the right-handed batsman it could be delivered by the bowler from a position right up against the stumps so that at the moment of delivery the ball actually came from the other side of the wicket. For this delivery I was always obliged to ensure that the umpire was standing well back, otherwise I would thump him in the back and there would be a no ball!

To the left-hander, the ball was delivered around the wicket, with "roundarm", so that at the point of delivery the arm was almost six feet from the stumps and with luck the ball would zip across the batsman. It was a quicker ball and, at times, very successful.

We had the double arm swinger — the arm whipping around twice, with a swinger's grip, hoping that the batsman would play a shot on the first whip and so be defenceless when the ball was actually released.

Then there was the leg-break. This could be followed by the "Groucho Marx" which simply consisted of a run up to the wicket with bent knees, so that instead of delivering at a height of, say seven feet, it was more like six and the ball was expected to hurry through.

Delivering about a yard back from the crease was another which, if combined with an early release, became a "flipper" and stayed longer in the air with a greater degree of spin. A more supple wrist might have produced a "googly", something I never achieved, but in later years the "flipper" has become a vital part of an old man's armoury with more top spin and higher flight path.

You meet all types of wicketkeeper. I have met some quite good keepers who, when I enquired, simply asked me to aim at their gloves. My most recent experience was with a delightful young man aged twelve who was called into the 2nd team at rather short notice and was probably about to keep to a spinner for the first time. I asked if he had kept to a spinner before and his confident reply was to the effect that he was a good keeper. Our opponents scored one hundred and sixty of which over forty were extras and the poor little lad suggested part way through that I give him some signals which left me scratching my head for most of the afternoon. I am sure he will make a first-class keeper and I have no doubt that he will seek me out when we next meet at nets.

And so it was with Clifford. Initially it had to be a very visual signal as finger signals over twenty-two yards were not always clear! We had to resort to a waving of a handkerchief. The batsmen were always taking pity on me for having a cold for the whole of the cricket season but it did not take them long to work out that every time I blew my nose, Clifford raced back about five yards!

Roy Parsons was another local product, a very fine sportsman indeed. Six feet three or so in height, he played soccer and was one of the best table tennis players ever to have graced the West. We called it "ping pong" but what he played was something else. I was asked to fill in one night for my local club and was drawn to play Roy. He turned up with a small case in which were his shorts and his own bat, something quite unheard of. His bat had rubber on both sides — I had sandpaper on one. Roy took it very easy on me and I marvelled at the number of times I did actually hit the ball, apparently past Roy and beneath the table, and his enormous arms would retrieve the ball and it would loop up from the floor, creep over the net and be spinning like a top. Roy had bucket hands, was a good opening bat with considerable power, and his round arm style of bowling from a great height made sure that the ball swung away, making him very difficult to hit. A great man to have in the side.

I have saved two rather special people until last. Peter Hawke, 'Awke to his friends, was one of the most intelligent, witty yet naive people I have ever been privileged to meet. Standing about six feet two inches in height, solidly built, he was an excellent cricketer, bowling quick left arm and he batted right-handed with a unique defensive shot which always left his right leg bent at the knee with his shinbone parallel to the ground. He saw things the others did not see, he was master of the funny situation and could exploit it, never causing offence and yet producing hilarious results. Probably a lonely man, he was a teacher, initially at Totnes Grammar, followed by a move to Camelford, just over the Cornish border. He lived for his cricket and Plymouth Argyle Football Club, both of which helped form a unique vocabulary which became part of the Westward Ho! folklore.

This might possibly be the place to mention his appropriate words for certain situations: *BPs* = Bonus points. We had a spell of playing friendlies but a local newspaper introduced BPs which did not improve the game. *NS* = Non serious. If a match finished early, we played NS to entertain the crowd. In other words, we made fools of ourselves. *Cack-handed* = A gentleman who batted left-handed. *L.B. Firkin* = Describing your dismissal if out leg before wicket. *Castled* = Bowled out, preferably by 'Awke. *Argee-hy-li-ho* = A loud chant from the stands at Plymouth Argyle by 'Awke and his merry band, sometimes boys on an outing from school. *Pen-naliteeee* = Advice to a referee at Argyle as to what decision should be given.

His classic was at one Cricket Club Annual Dinner when he was called on to propose a toast to "The Worshipful the Mayor", Mrs Ethelwynne Brown, and forgot her name, eventually calling her "Mrs Thing-a-me-bob". Mrs Brown took this extremely well and when she came again the following year, Peter introduced her as "Mrs Thing-a-me-bob" — she was delighted.

The final mention (there will be others who joined us later) is of Mervyn Bird. A great friend, Mervyn was a one off. The biggest leg-puller I have known, a supreme batsman who never bothered to net, nothing worried him, and he could turn his hand to most things. His squat figure five feet nine inches in height, a massive fifty-three inch chest, and seventeen stones in weight, indicated a prop forward, a county one at that. He was the best snooker player for miles (if Joe Davis, the world champion, was to give an exhibition in the area, Mervyn was the man called to oppose him) and on a tennis court he was a handful with exquisite positioning and a gentle touch. I did hear that he did have a go at golf and he played the first nine holes at The Royal North Devon Golf Course (an extremely difficult course for the novice) in par — I for one would not doubt that, Mervyn's ball sense was tremendous. Having scored a century one Saturday, he told me he would go for it again on the Sunday, and he did. He could read bowlers and there were some who could move the ball both ways, but somehow he would know. When I did bowl to him in the nets (the very odd occasion) I would come in to bowl off four paces and as soon as I turned to approach the wicket, he could shout out what I was intending to bowl to him. His achievements were mostly on poorish wickets and had he been given a chance at higher level, I am sure he would have succeeded as his technique was so good, coupled with immense power.

What I have perhaps not stressed enough, was that there were many characters in the team so that spirits never had a chance to fall and there was always strength to come whether in the field or batting. We traded on this for a good many years giving enjoyment to the many who found their way to Westward Ho! on Saturday and Sunday afternoons simply to watch the cricket.

This was the first season that North Devon had encountered a genuine leg spinner who could bowl a googly. Les Bircumshaw, a teacher who came down to North Devon for his summer holidays, found the Instow ground very much to his liking and from July until the end of August, would rattle up a thousand runs and mesmerise the opposition with his well disguised deliveries.

Robbie (who played for both Bideford and North Devon) witnessed many a grand performance by Les so that when the two sides met, Robbie opted to play for Bideford. We were briefed before batting and clearly told that the googly was virtually impossible to spot but when we heard Les snap his fingers "Never mind what thou thinks, lad, 'tis a googly" confided Robbie in his broadest Yorkshire dialect. The team coped quite well and eventually went on to win but last man, Cliff Cudmore went in, the ball pitched a foot outside the off stump, Cliff shouldered arms and was "castled". Robbie hadn't reckoned on Cliff being a little deaf!

Sam Pidler was in his element at this time. Sam, a painter and decorator by trade, was a hard-hitting bat and medium paced seamer, and probably the best wet ball bowler I have known. His central parting and Brylcreemed hair were also impressive and in addition to being the midweek captain, he also turned out at weekends to good effect. One of his major achievements was scoring one hundred and fourteen runs against Lynton as part of an opening stand of one hundred and eighty-four with Ray Bird. I shall never forget his supreme confidence in bowling a Whimple and Whiteways opening bat with the last ball of an over. Sam quickly summed this up by telling me that he had spotted the batsman's weakness right away and as a result had bowled him "five inswingers and then the outswinger". And to think I had always thought of him as a "straight up and down bowler"!

1954 — Every season seemed to be memorable for some reason or other and it was in 1954 that Mervyn Bird joined the club. This gave us a regular left-handed No.3, a virtual run-machine, great friend and personality. He was soon to make his mark.

Fairly early in the season, Robbie hit one hundred and seventy-eight runs against tourists Polytechnic CC, including sixteen sixes. I was secretary at the time and arrived at the ground later in the day to be met by persons wishing to claim off our insurers. Several balls had gone straight through the roofs of the adjoining bungalows and as many did not have accesses to the roof space, cricket balls in the roof space soon became a feature.

It was about this time that I began to take note of umpires. North Devon clubs were very well blessed in this department and I have always regarded the umpire as being a very vital part of any game. Without them the games would not be so enjoyable, but some had their own little ways!

One of the first situations I recall was at a match played at Braunton when a most respected umpire was standing. The ball was turning and the opening bat shouldered arms on or about the off stump to a ball pitching about two feet outside. The ball whipped back, the bails flew, the batsman was in a trance and I was elated. No one moved where upon I enquired "How was that?" The umpire's vision might have been somewhat obscured but he had the presence of mind to assemble his thoughts and come out with the splendid assessment "Not out — impossible!" I didn't get a wicket but somehow I felt that I had achieved the impossible!

A distinguished ex-Army captain joined us as umpire at or about this time — a truly splendid addition complete with sun blind blazer and shooting stick. Copey had played cricket to quite a good standard in his time and he enjoyed every minute of every game, so much so that for the last game of the season he invariably wore a black top hat and went into mourning! He had his very high standards which may, at times, have taken preference over the laws of this venerable game. Coloured socks were an anathema and woe betide anyone coming out to bat exhibiting such ill-chosen accoutrements, the faintest notion of ball hitting pad and the tasteless batter would be on his way back from whence he had cometh. Copey also carried the smallest of bottles of iodine which, if ever a batsman was struck by the ball wherever the point of contact, Copey would offer his elixir as the sure solution.

This was the year when the County Cricket Club took the revolutionary step of importing an experienced captain, Graham Parker, a university blue who had also played for Gloucestershire in the County Championship. Graham, a very capable all-rounder, was instrumental in arranging a series of Club and Ground games in various parts of the county to see what talent was available. The Club and Ground game involving North Devon was to be played at Barnstaple on the old Raleigh Ground, long since developed. Club and Ground would bring along a side with a sprinkling of players with Minor Counties experience to test the local up-and-comers.

My cherished mode of transport since leaving school had been a Hercules Kestrel bicycle, painted gold with a three speed gear, and a dynamo to provide me with the faintest of light for night riding. Each day it hastened my trip to the office, we cycled away to football matches (sometimes nine miles away before the game itself) and twice a week during the summer I would cycle the three miles to Westward Ho! for net practice and then again for games. My kit (such as it was) neatly fitted into Grandad's brown carrier bag slung on one arm.

Being in regular employment (I had changed to local government following National Service) and with the eventual prospect of a pension, I decided it was time to splash out on a more advanced form of transport and chose a second-hand motorbike which a chap in the adjoining office was anxious to get rid of. It seemed silly to me that one could buy such a machine, stick on L-plates and obtain insurance and away you could go without any training or experience. Presumably the L-plates kept most sensible people out of the way.

The one thing which mystified me was the whereabouts of the hooter. In this case it was in the shape of a klaxon-type horn, hidden beneath the seat. What a stupid idea! The first lengthy ride I undertook was to Hartland, a quiet rural area, and as I was going along a country lane I rounded a corner to be confronted by a herd of sheep all over the road, leaving no passageway. I hastened to locate my hooter, missed it first time and ended up unseated in the midst of sheep. No one was hurt and the sheep seemed to enjoy the incident. How stupid — I decided there and then to relocate the hooter to make it more accessible. Firmly fixed on the handlebars for all to see, I felt much more aware and was genuinely prepared for all eventualities — until it rained! What should have been a warning signal ended up with a spurt of water which although an attractive feature, did little in the warning stakes.

As Mervyn Bird and his seventeen stones lived at Northam on my way to the ground, I invariably gave him a lift. It was asking much of a 197cc two stroke engine, but it was all down hill except that Mervyn had more control over the machine than I had. He would sit on the back with his cricket bag across his knees, my carrier bag was on the petrol tank and off we would go. Down over the hill to Sandymere Road and then a sharp turning to the left along Golf Links Road. It was invariably at this point that Mervyn would simply twist his knees to the right, no way could I turn to the left and we would go sailing on to the Burrows!

The same arrangement was made for the trip to Barnstaple, Mervyn having been a No.1 choice and I had limped in when another player withdrew. It is rather different playing in a selected XI, where most are strangers, and the familiarity is missing. One or two of the Devon lads were in a class of their own and the local XI vainly chased a higher target than they were perhaps used to. We changed in silence, my performance had not merited a wicket and the whole match was probably best forgotten. I made my way to my sandy coloured "Tanden" (I have never heard of that make before or since) and awaited Mervyn. He duly arrived with the message "Graham Parker is looking for you."

I thought immediately — Mervyn never loses his sense of humour and is leg pulling again. "Jump on Mervyn, blow Graham Parker (or the equivalent)."

Mervyn tried to emphasise the fact and I attacked

the kick-start with gusto only to find Graham Parker at my elbow before you could say "goggles". "I'd like to see more of you — will you play at Sidmouth next month?"

1955 — This was the year the team acquired "a cutting edge". Martin Wheatley, a swiftish bowler from the Home Counties whose father became mine host of a local hostelry. After sorting out the troubles in Singapore, which was accompanied by a medal for fighting in NAAFI queues, Martin joined the local electricity authority to begin an illustrious career. His first write-up prompted the prime reporter to record that *"Wheatley accounted for the two openers with his pacey deliveries, some of which he swung* (this was news to Martin) *but most of which gained their venom by virtue of their speed off the turf"*. This was followed shortly afterwards by *"Whirlwind Wheatley strikes again"*.

The message got through to Tommy Down, an illustrious cricketer with Barnstaple. Tommy was a man of the soil, down to earth — cricket was all about speed, bowl as fast as you can, hit as hard as you can. He was a man of few words but he usually greeted me by saying "I like playing against you, you'm rubbish." Tom never lacked confidence! Very often his innings would be prefixed by "Take it easy, I have been very ill since last year" and the likelihood was that the next ball would rattle the fence. And so it was with Whirlwind Wheatley. Tom opened the batting that day and as he passed me he said "Which one's Whirlwind Wheatley?" I pointed to Martin shortening his run up to accommodate the boundary. A particularly vicious delivery sped from Martin's high action, Tommy and bat became a blur, and there was the umpire signalling a six. What happened thereafter was of little consequence, Tommy had done what he had set out to achieve. No one ever challenged Tom's weaponry. His bat appeared bound with a particular class of copper wire and under close scrutiny it might not have been willow being very dark brown in colour. It worked, that was the main thing,

"Whirlwind Wheatley strikes again!"

and both Tom and the bat were fearless.

It may be said that at times "Wheaters" was indirectly assisted by the umpire. He certainly was one of Copey's favourites probably because he was more likely to cause injury than anyone else and the iodine could come into play.

More than once I have seen Bideford take the field with a modest one hundred and twenty or so on the board so that all stops would have to be pulled out to get a win. Martin would go back his twenty or so paces, the opening batsman would take his guard and Copey would shout "Play" allowing two seconds before extending his right arm to the side stopping Martin in his tracks. Copey would then sedately walk down to the wicket to the opening bat and enquire "You have got a box on, old man, this chap's bloody fast." Somehow Martin had a knack for getting early wickets!

1956 — Roy Bird, the third and youngest of the Bird brothers, joined the club and was welcomed as an away-swing bowler, powerful batter and with probably the fastest pair of hands I have seen when it came to close catching.

We were building up a good all-round team with batters and bowlers interchangeable and the fielding improved considerably with a leg trap being frequently employed. At one stage, this reached almost stupid proportions when there was invariably a race by the local fielding side to take up a short fielding position on the leg side where there was sure to be some action.

This was not necessarily the best position to be in when "Two spin" Bill Shortridge was in confident mood as his "Leggers" simply went higher and higher. Wednesday, 15th August, 1956, could well have been the pinnacle of his illustrious career. The visitors were Sun of Canada, a well known insurance company, whose ranks included former England captain R. E. S. Wyatt, and J. Fleming, a former cricket captain of Scotland. What a challenge for Bill! Whirling away up the slope, with a tantalising mixture of off-breaks and leg-breaks, Bill bamboozled both, clean bowling Wyatt for fifty (he was heard to say "Which way did that go!") and Fleming for an attractive twenty. Bill celebrated afterwards with a few shandies at the local Conservative Club, and 'Awke, who was delighted to enlarge upon this impressive feat by his good friend announced to all and sundry "Never mind about having to bowl up the slope, I would bowl 'Hagan' up Everest!" You could see Bill's chest going out as he relished every word.

At or about that time, one of the best local all-rounders was one Dougie Jones of Lynton. A tall elegant batsman, Doug also bowled a useful medium pace and if a representative side was ever chosen, Doug was usually first on the list. Bill was frightened of no one, regarding most as lesser mortals who occasionally had a lucky day, and the fireman's belt holding up his trousers was something of a sign of his authority on the cricket field. Whenever we played against Lynton and assembled in the changing room, 'Awke would say to Bill "Dougie telephoned last night to ask if you were playing, he is quite worried about having to face you." Bill took in every word, genuinely believing that Dougie was extremely worried at the prospect of having to face him and so when Bill was asked to bowl, he exuded confidence and the game was as good as won.

I remember one such happening at the beautiful "Valley of the Rocks" ground where Lynton played their home matches. It is a glorious setting with very high hills with rocky outcrops on two sides, and it has subsequently been acknowledged as one of the prettiest club grounds in the country if not the world. At the time it had a small, delightful thatched pavilion much too small for all the team to change at once but this added to the attraction of something so beautiful and unique. It was perfect in such a setting but sadly, in later years, it attracted the attention of an arsonist.

Dougie came in to bat very early on and 'Awke reminded Bill of the phone call. Two or three very high floaters followed (Doug would not hit these, he would use them as sighters) and then the faster off-break.

Doug lunged forward, missed, lost his balance and fell forward onto the ground in front of the approaching Bill following through. It was an easy stumping and with Dougie still lying prostrate, Bill looked down, wagged his forefinger and said "You never could play the off-break Dougie." 'Awke was triumphant knowing full well that his psychology had worked once again.

It was this season that Mervyn Bird became the first Bideford batsman since the war to reach a thousand runs in a season and the last North Devon batsman to perform that feat had been Doug Jones, seven seasons earlier. These were certainly great times with performances perhaps somewhat modest when compared to later events.

1957 — One of the memorable things about the "old days" was the fact that invariably the players were the club and whilst the cricket ground at Westward Ho! was a focal point at weekends, most of "the Committee" were, in fact, the players themselves and as such were responsible for balancing the books, ground preparation and maintenance. In 1956 the annual rent was £40 which was increased in 1957 to £60. The secretary announced that "providing petrol rationing did not affect travelling facilities", we could be assured of another good season with over sixty games arranged.

This was the year when "League" cricket was unofficially introduced and without rules, it proved something of a disaster. Three points were to be awarded for an outright win, one point each for a draw and nothing if a team lost. 'Awke immediately coined new phraseology and "BPs" became the order of the day — bonus points.

The Bideford CC did quite well but against one struggling side visiting Westward Ho! clearly illustrated that just playing for BPs was not the answer and that if there was to be a league, then it should have proper rules.

The normal Saturday fixture began at 2.30 p.m. and the side batting first could bat until tea (5 p.m.). There was little leverage here as teas were taken in a nearby restaurant and tables had to be reserved for the players. With luck, the first side batting could enjoy two and a half hours at the wicket, whereas the team batting second would have from 5.30 p.m. until 7.30 p.m. All went reasonably well until a struggling side arrived just after 3 p.m. and took thirty minutes to change into appropriate cricketing attire. Bideford batted first, the openers going out at 3.30 p.m. knowing full well that we would be sitting down to tea just after 5 p.m. In the intervening period, the home side amassed one hundred and twenty runs, hardly enough in normal circumstances but if BPs and the "League" were considered important, then a bold declaration was the only answer. An intrepid skipper boldly took the step and by 5.30 p.m. the visitors started the chase.

At 7 p.m. the visitors were getting into desperate straits, the ninth wicket had fallen, there was no hope, but the visiting captain thought otherwise. 'Awke was doing rather well with his left arm quickies from the bottom end and fancied the No.11. He took his first stride towards the trembling No.11 just as the visiting captain came onto the field from the pavilion shouting "I appeal against the light. I appeal against the rain. I appeal against the heat. I appeal against everything."

'Awke did not break in his stride but kept going, a whirl of the arm, a clatter of wickets followed by "Castled" at full volume, and at a slightly lesser number of decibels "Appeal against that!" We all felt sorry for the visiting skipper who was virtually pushed out of the pavilion by his team mates in a last vain attempt to get one BP but it was not to be.

Many, many years later, I encountered John Fry, a stalwart of the Braunton CC, who kept wicket and was a very useful batsman. John subsequently went on to umpire at a very good level, but with the advent of Devon League Cricket (and possibly the influence of overseas players), the game became very much harder and slagging the batsman became an unfair way of unsettling a batsman, almost before he had taken his guard. Subsequently in the League we have had suspensions and in the case of a current Australian Test cricketer, his season ended prematurely due to suspension for politely describing a batsman's ability with the willow! At any level, this cannot add anything to the game, is unfair, is uncouth, and has no place on the village green.

I well remember John recalling that the worst case of slagging off during his career as a player was when he came to the wicket against Bideford, in an almost irretrievable position, and was confronted by 'Awke who said "Cometh the hour, cometh the man!"

The midweek team at Bideford consisted mostly of businessmen in the town at a time when the half-day was a Wednesday and most shops closed on that day. There was not much of a choice but nevertheless there were quite a number of useful players and when the opposition was considerably above par (we did act as hosts to quite a number of excellent touring sides) some of the weekend players would make themselves available and there were always students about during the summer holidays.

One midweek fixture at that time was West Buckland School. They had a particularly fine side with a batsman from Plymouth who was subsequently destined to play for the county and a particularly good fast bowler by the name of Bickley. Word quickly went around when someone special had arrived in this part of the world and this young man was certainly making a name for himself. In two matches, he took sixteen wickets with some very quick, accurate bowling but he cost us our star all-rounder Alf Robinson, for the rest of the season. He struck Robbie on the box which Robbie had not put on properly and so not all of him was protected. The blow was as serious as it was painful.

The event was recalled at our annual Dinner Dance, when various presentations were made, and our president, Copey the umpire, duly obliged with the opening speech which was made after sherry, wine and liqueur. The situation wasn't helped by Copey dropping his false teeth into a bowl of trifle which he deigned to find himself rather than involve the waitress, and then he launched into his long awaited speech on the success (or otherwise) of the season. When he came to Robbie, our star all-rounder, he recounted how well Robbie had been playing, taking wickets and scoring runs until that fateful day at West Buckland when he faced the full fury of young Buckley only to be hit in the b.... Copey quickly realised he could not finish what he had originally intended to say what with The Worshipful The Mayor Mrs Ethelwynne Brown sitting alongside, and quickly adjusted and stammered "only to be struck." He realised he was on the same tack and hastily added "Well, if he had been a lady, he wouldn't have been hit at all!"

This year was made all the more interesting by a very convincing win at the end of the season over North Devon. Six batsmen got ducks and of the visitors' total of fifty-five, thirty-two runs were scored by sixteen-year-old David Shepherd. This was the beginning of a lengthy association with this future Gloucester county player and international umpire which continues to this day.

Almost the last game of the season was a benefit match for Ray Illingworth (Yorkshire and England) and Cliff Gladwin (Derbyshire and England). At that time an end of season Torquay Cricket Festival was held, both sides comprising professional players of some standing and it was usual for Barton CC to visit us and bring along some of the professionals providing an opportunity for the North Devon supporters to see cricketers of the highest standard whilst they, in turn, were permitted to "take the hat around", chat to the spectators and generally make the occasion. Barton were expected to provide the entertainment and so were given first knock. Ray Illingworth came in at No.3 and delighted us for a while but according to the local press *"Jared beat him with a beauty"* and he was bowled for twenty-two. All was going quite well until Cliff Gladwin came in. Jim Dickenson, another county man, had gone and Cliff immediately introduced himself to me. "Aye lad, I've played for England, I've taken plenty of wickets, I know what I am talking about. If I were thee, I would bowl around the wicket, pack the leg side, you'll run through us."

"I'm happy as I am."

"Nay, lad, I know, I played for England......" He obviously realised that the leg side boundary was extremely short and the merest tickle would be a four but he was rather persistent. I was pressed into accepting his "helpful" advice — a lousy bat, he was the highest scorer on his side, but we had a good laugh about it afterwards.

The event attracted one of the largest crowds ever seen at the Westward Ho! ground and in those days it was not uncommon to see the crowd two or three thick along the top fence with cars and deck chairs around the other three sides. They were great days.

Initially when becoming a club cricketer, it was a case of batting at No.11 until you scored more runs than No.10 and then perhaps you might go up one. It was much the same with the ball, most people brought their arm over and so at best, unless you were aspiring to be a very quick bowler, you started as fourth or fifth change. What a joy it was, therefore, to enjoy fielding. Some people have a fairly good "arm", some can throw considerable distances, but I found very early on, that from cover point, I could whizz the ball in low and fast. Being young and reasonably quick in the field, this became part of the game. I could stand in a cover point position to challenge the batsmen — make them think there could be a run but there was just the off chance that a quick move in to the ball, sure pick up and throw "off the ground" might make me the winner by an inch or two. This type of throwing action does not seem to curry favour with present day coaches who encourage the "stand up and point" approach but there must be exceptions. The word does get around, however.

The September weather was glorious and RP, a splendid sportsman from Torrington, agreed to raise a side to play an extra fixture at Westward Ho! This was a splendid gesture to us, the crowd would enjoy it and it would shorten the winter. When it came time for Torrington to bat, the opener with the jazz hat was at the non-striker's end. In addition to being the local banker, he was also a star attraction and looking to do well in front of such a large crowd. I took up my usual position — not too deep, not too close, but ready for the quick pick up. The first ball was well pitched up, called for a defensive prod which was directed towards my position. The anxious batsman, wishing to get off the mark, called for a run. I was well on my way, collected the ball on the edge of the square, flashed it to the top of the stumps just as the batsmen were crossing. The bails came off, howzat, on your bike without facing. The walk back to the pavilion was slow and meaningful. The gloves were taken off and from about ten feet were hurled over the single storey pavilion and into the holiday chalets beyond. The two steps into the pavilion must have felt like mountains and from the pitch we could hear the cricket bat sailing around the dressing room, bouncing off one wall then another. It was nearly the end of the game when calmness prevailed and the opener felt inclined to look for his gloves. Needless to say, they were never found!

In August, Harold Stephenson had a benefit match which was played at Ilfracombe between an Ilfracombe XII and a North Devon XII. It provided the locals with an opportunity of seeing such splendid players such as Peter Wight (Somerset), Colin McCool (Australia and Somerset), Harold himself, and John McMahon (Surrey). Brian Roe (Somerset) also played for the North Devon side. I have a number of happy memories of that game. Firstly, having watched Peter Wight from the boundary at Taunton, I marvelled at how such a slight frame could propel a ball with such speed to the nearest boundary. Bowling to him was an absolute education — he seemed to be able to drive anything and with massive power. It took batting to a new level. I was able to account for Chris Greetham (Somerset) and was delighted to have a new face to bowl to, Harold

"The gloves were taken off and from about ten feet were hurled over the single storey pavilion . . ."

Stephenson.

Harold was perhaps unfortunate in that he was a superb wicketkeeper but had little chance of national honours whilst England could still call on the excellent and undisputed Godfrey Evans. This was not my problem and having struggled against Wight and McCool, I was anxious to cash in (if at all possible) on the lesser mortals to come. Harold was not too sure of himself on a wicket which was beginning to turn and the first thing he did was to shuffle across in front of his wicket and to try and play the turning ball off the pitch. This was OK as long as he kept hitting the ball, but a miss and he should have been on his way. He did this a couple of times and I thought, this is it, time for the "Miller roundarm". A slow approach to the wicket, I could almost see Harold relaxing, and the arm came over in a blur and the faster ball pinned him right back on to his stumps. Harold was not quite sure what was happening, the non-striker called for a run, I appealed frantically for a certain LBW. Copey, our umpire, had been waiting for this moment all afternoon — a chance to speak to the second best wicketkeeper in England. "Dashed bad luck, Harold, Godfrey's in such fine form!" My appeal was ignored — it would have made a young man's afternoon.

Rain off the channel brought the game to an early halt and we all changed in the same, not too large, room. My carrier bag and its few contents had disappeared only to be found ten minutes or so later in the corner of John McMahon's rather large professional bag which was about half the size of the bags and boxes used by our colts players of today. How things have changed!

1958 — AGMs were quite an event and an impressive profit on the previous year's workings of £103 was recorded but it would be necessary for visitors to pay for their own teas in future. The president's contribution was that "this was done all over England and by the

MCC" — who were we to argue!

Cliff Cudmore, our wicketkeeper for many years who depended very much upon hand signals from his bowler as to what and where the next delivery was likely to be, was not as well as we would have hoped but this made way for a promising young keeper, Andy, who was to feature for many, many years to come. Andy lived just up the road from the cricket field and he virtually spent all his spare hours at the ground, a very good attribute for any aspiring young player. What he lacked in initial ability he more than made up for with his tremendous determination and his coming was to be the forming of a very long friendship which continues to this day.

And so the season was beginning to take shape with the prospect of the local authority being approached for a grant towards the provision of a practice wicket. The usual practice was for nets to be erected each practice evening, rather in boy scout fashion, with poles, ropes and stakes, on an area which was reasonably level and had the benefit of a roll or two by a very light hand roller after a brief trim by a hand propelled lawn mower. Thereafter, most players sought to hit the ball as far as they possibly could. Cricket balls had to be shared and there was no suggestion of coaching or trying to improve, it was more a case of "keeping your hand in".

On the question of hands, this was the first occasion that the local side did combat with Filleigh who had introduced a man of the soil, Tom Leach, as their opening bowler. Tom was a very likeable man, big and brawny with extremely large hands so much so that in all our subsequent encounters, I never saw him wear batting gloves — no one made them large enough! As much as a bowler tried to rap his knuckles, the bat always seemed to get there first!

Looking back over the fixture lists, the away games were played at the beginning and at the end of a season, and very often we would alternate visiting North Cornwall at Bude at the beginning of one season with the return game at Westward Ho! in September, and vice versa.

This year, our away fixture came first. Ray Bird, our captain, opened the batting and, after an early loss of a wicket, he was joined by brother Mervyn and both mounted a joint assault on the beleaguered North Cornwall bowlers, including Mr Littlejohns, who got hammered whilst collecting two wickets. I recall he also missed a catch. Later, chasing one hundred and eighty-five runs to win, the Cornish wickets began to fall at regular intervals and in walked Mr Littlejohns. His stay was of minimal duration — he failed to score — and trudged back into the wooden pavilion, sited on the hillock overlooking the ground. No sooner had he disappeared from view than there was a tremendous bang (it could have been a car nearby, they did those things in those days!). Mervyn immediately turned to me and said "Poor sod, I didn't realise he took his cricket so seriously!"

Touring sides were always keen to come to Westward Ho! and it became quite a problem in ensuring that the home sides were strong enough to compete with some very good opposition. The problem was addressed by having a Festival Cricket Week (in true Devon fashion it lasted nine days) which enabled players to take some holiday and ensure that fairly balanced sides took the field. It was interesting playing on a daily basis as performance had to be tempered with the drain on stamina and aching fingers (particularly if you were a bowler). I was delighted that my tally of wickets rose by thirty-seven in the week, something which now takes me two or three seasons!

The end of the season was fast approaching and Barton CC from Torquay were due to visit once again — who would their guests be this time? Ray Illingworth decided to come again and he was accompanied by Brian Close. Several hundred spectators watched the game and they were not disappointed by the England stars who each scored a century. In addition they took nine wickets between them.

Despite the fact that it may have been "a friendly",

there was no such thing in the BC handbook and all matches by their very nature had to be competitive. Keeping wicket that day was young Andy — what a thrill to be playing against two all time "greats". He even bought a new bat for the occasion. Bideford did not fare too well against the combined spin and pace attack of the two internationals, and the time soon came for Andy to take his place at the wicket to retrieve an almost impossible situation. Having taken his guard, Andy made up his mind that they would not pass, no matter who the bowlers were, and runs did not really matter. The first ball down the slope from Close wizzed past the outside edge and Close held his head in dismay. The next ball moved the other way but Andy played straight to defend his wicket and missed the ball by miles. More histrionics by BC but Andy was still there. BC deciding the leg cutter was probably the best bet, fizzed down another — Andy played straight, missed and first slip fielded the ball. BC was virtually steaming by this time, Andy was probably trembling but he had decided to stand his ground, his luck had to change. The fourth ball was a snorter, leg and middle taking off. Andy covered it got an edge and the ball hit the boundary whilst the slips were still clutching air. "You lucky sod (or something similar)" added colour to the moment of BC's extreme disappointment but Andy decided this was the moment to actually speak to the great man on a one to one basis. "Sorry, Mr. Close, but I did buy the edge with the rest of the bat." I am sure BC had a gentle chuckle to himself.

I was actually away at the time of the game but Ray did ask after me, recalling the duel which we had enjoyed the previous year with both bat and ball. I was over the moon that he had remembered the game amongst so many others — perhaps the sign of a very great sportsman.

I subsequently met BC once again. He was the principal speaker at a celebration evening arranged by a local cricket club and I was due to be the second speaker. We exchanged pleasantries, he recalled his superb performance at Westward Ho! and he then proceeded to ramble on until after midnight to an increasingly restless audience, and looking at my watch, I could see the time slipping away as were some of my audience. At least he was being paid!

1959 — The opening comment for the year was to the effect that the New Year's Eve Dance could not be held as no suitable local dance band was available. This prompted much thought within the club — more about this later!

Collections were down to £142, a drop of 43% on the 1955 figure! Going around with a box on Sundays was a feature of every home game but not so popular amongst the players. Rattling the box at people leaning over the fence was quite a feat and to extract a few pence or even six pence usually called for a lengthy stop and chat and a fair amount of abuse from the knowledgeable regulars on the top fence, particularly those by the sightscreen who had a grandstand view. The worst scenario was when you were an early batsman, not troubling the scorers on the day, and all regular fans demanded a detailed explanation of your downfall and what they would have done had they been given half a chance! It seemed to take hours to go around the whole ground but I well remember that Close and Illingworth were delighted to do so the previous season, sharing the proceeds and pocketing £9 each — a fair day's work then, but not so in today's terms.

Economies would have to be effected and the weekend teams would have to travel "by private conveyance with members being reimbursed". The deck chairs which had been on sale on Sundays belonged to the local Council which was not satisfied with the sharing of the amount collected by the club, suggesting that a greater effort should have been made by the club. One club member suggested that "caps had been left alongside the stack of chairs into which the money should have been placed, but people had helped themselves to the chairs without payment". Nothing changes. The club decided to buy some chairs of its own. At the same meeting, it was pointed out that the club had no proper rules or constitution. In retrospect, I wonder how many clubs did.

This year was also a personal turning point. It seemed that I had always had bladder problems doubtless brought about by a certain nervousness with the thought of having to bat. With this in mind, a clear indication as to the batting order was a must to allow plenty of time for all pre-batting formalities. If you were in the top four, the order of priorities was plain, a visit to the toilet prior to padding up in which case we were reasonably assured unless there was a fairly substantial stand (twenty or so plus) at the beginning of the innings. This might involve a further visit, partial disrobing, and hopefully a few minutes afterwards to gain one's composure. The problem at Westward Ho! was that the public toilets had to be used and they were fronting onto the public highway on the top side of the ground. This was some one hundred yards from the wooden pavilion with seated spectators along one side with the fence leaners on the top fence. At times, it seemed much further than one hundred yards.

It was with particular personal pleasure, therefore, that the Northam Council decided (despite opposition from a number of members!) that it should advance to the cricket club £90 or 50%, whichever was the less, towards the cost of installing lavatories at the ground, adjoining the wooden pavilion, so aptly referred to as "The Hutch" by my ever-loving wife. The Council's debate was furious, expending such a colossal amount for a club with only six years to run on the current lease, but someone who subsequently turned out to be a splendid personal friend, with words of great wisdom announced that he "Applauded those who devoted their time to provide good entertainment at Westward Ho!" And contended that "The Council should give the club every encouragement and assistance. This," he said, "was an essential amenity." It certainly was for me!

Such inconveniences (or maybe lack of conveniences) caused untold problems on some of the more rustic grounds. Raleigh CC from Barnstaple played on the playing fields attached to a local girls' convent and the wooden pavilion in one corner of the ground was used by the school children (boys and girls) during the week and by the cricketers at weekends. It was a very pleasant ground to play on but the toilets were somewhat limited in their application in that there was a urinal at the entrance and a cubicle around the back with outside approach. Presumably the latter was solely for the use of the young ladies but the inner workings of one's body did not always legislate for such ill-conceived utilities.

On this particular day, I found myself in the lower echelons of the batting order but still one above my formidable friend "Whirlwind Wheatley". Robbie was going extremely well with the bat on what turned out to be a sunny afternoon, so much so that not having a cap with him, he utilised the handkerchief in his pocket by tying a knot in each corner and firmly affixing it to his head and sweating brow. Robbie was going well — too well in his estimation — and on the warmest day of the summer asked for his long-sleeved sweater to slow him down as he started to play a few rash shots!

The time was obviously approaching when I might be required to replace Robbie or yet his partner and my inner body reminded me that a visit to the toilet was necessary. The urinal was of little use and after a quick recce, "Wheaters" decided that I should use the ladies and he would stand guard outside. This seemed a very sensible suggestion in the light of ever pressing circumstances and with a firm assurance from my friend that he would repel all those brave enough to approach the ladies, I proceeded about my pressing business. There were occasional reassurances between us as he stood guard, and then, all of a sudden, nothing. Robbie had holed out, "Wheaters" could see an opportunity not to be missed and without a moment's hesitation, he donned his batting gloves, picked up his bat, and strode out to meet the foe. I emerged shortly afterwards, totally embarrassed at my possible exposure, my guard having left his post, but doubly hurt to see that he had usurped my batting position and was scoring freely!

It was rare that we played away from Westward Ho! once the season started as most clubs relished the idea of playing cricket on a seaside ground with only a pebble ridge between it and the Atlantic. There was always a refreshing breeze, a good crowd and the prospect of obtaining a sun tan from the wind if not the sun. Coupled with the playing of cricket, it was really a very happy place to be on a good weekend.

One of the rare excursions was to Dulverton, just over the Somerset border and on the edge of Exmoor. In May, the display of rhododendrons was second to none, the hillsides overlooking the cricket ground yielding a magnificent display. One of their stars was Arthur Chanter, the village blacksmith, with arms like tree trunks. He was one of the hardest hitters of the ball I had ever seen and as a keeper he was like greased lightning, but for every stumping there were usually a few extras.

By this time Father Christmas had brought me what should have been a cricket bag but my mother mistakenly had been persuaded to purchase a hockey bag — possibly similar but with the narrowest of slots on the outside to slide in a hockey stick but little else. Not to be outdone, and certainly not wishing to upset my mother, I sawed off the handle of an old bat so that this could protrude from my new "cricket bag". The only thing was, I had to carry the real bat in my bag with the rest of my kit, not a very sensible thing to do when we were constantly reminded that we should keep our bats well oiled with linseed oil to get the best out of them. It was then that Roy Bird came to my aid. Being a salesman with an agricultural merchants, he was constantly selling manure and the like to farmers and it so happened that Fisons No.4, a British fertiliser, was sold in transparent plastic bags which could be reduced in size and restitched to provide an ideal cover for a linseeded bat. The cricket/hockey bag was still sizeable enough to cover the entire bat, thank goodness.

Now it so happened that the dressing rooms at Dulverton led directly off the central hall where tea was to be taken. It is not unusual when batters are going in and out for a dressing room to become an absolute tip in no time at all and when called upon to bat in a bit of a hurry, it is the easiest thing in the world to pick up one's bat, take off and discard the cover and then stride manfully to the wicket. This I did rather hastily when two or three wickets fell in quick succession. When I eventually returned to the pavilion, it was suggested that one of the tea ladies had walked past our dressing room with open door, seen a rather large transparent sheath on the floor and had fainted! I never actually heard the end of the story but I still carry the Fisons No.4 cover to this very day.

Our matches with North Devon were always keenly fought and something which was savoured by the better players. Here again, the pitch at Instow is magnificent, bounded on one side by the confluence of the Rivers Taw and Torridge and the pavilion is a listed building of cob and stone with glorious thatched roof. The smaller scorer's hut is in similar vein. The playing area is large to county standard and somehow one's whole game had to be adjusted to cater for extra large boundaries and so much space. Fielding positions had to be varied, the wicket was good, the kudos of winning immense.

It was at or about this time that we varied our wicketkeepers and Peter Williams, who likened himself to Tom Graveney, but was short and tubby and froze when confronted by a spinner, often stood in. A great character, a batsman with several hundreds to his name, and even a hat trick with high flying leg-breaks, he was certainly a useful all-rounder and no fool behind the stumps. Things seemed to be going reasonably well for the visitors who had batted first and had been

"... one of the tea ladies had walked past our dressing room, seen a rather large transparent sheath on the floor and had fainted!"

persuaded by the guardian of the gong that tea was ready and we should declare. Peter W was reluctant and asked for a few more overs but still the guardian of the gong was poised with drumstick raised. In the end, Peter W gave in, the gong was struck a resounding blow signifying tea to everyone in the ground and most of the people on the adjoining seafront. The only thing was that when we had finished tea, we realised that tea had been taken about half an hour early giving the home side a distinct advantage after tea! Had the captain had a watch we would certainly have carried on for the extra thirty minutes.

This was not the end of the captain's embarrassing day. The wicket at Instow gives a little encouragement to the bowler, but in the main it is the batsmen who derive the greatest pleasure in stroking the ball around this vast field. Wickets are therefore hard to come by. Peter W was keeping quite immaculately and the ball was turning a little, sufficient to cause some of the later batsmen a bit of bother. A little wind assistance off the river and some wearing patches offered encouragement and Bideford got stuck in and were beginning to make inroads. The match ended in a draw with the home side requiring thirteen more runs with two wickets in hand — probably a fair result in a keenly contested game, but it could easily have gone the way of the visitors, when the spinning ball beat the bat of an outstretched batsman who dragged his rear foot. Peter W had the bails off in a flash, possibly the fastest he has ever moved, to delicately remove the bails with the batsman's foot on the line. "Howzat" came the chorus — a magnificent piece of work by any standards. All eyes turned towards the square leg umpire.

"Not out" came the firm reply.

"Has to be the same day!" It was one of those times when one thinks, if only I had thought of that. The beer flowed well that night.

We continued to put out a Wednesday side comprising local businessmen who in those days invariably closed their shops and establishments for the afternoon as Wednesday was early closing day. These matches did not quite carry the same amount of intensity as the weekend games but nevertheless were most enjoyable. I remember my first such encounter with Werrington from over the Cornwall border, which fielded a team with three members bearing the same family name and all competent performers. What I did not bargain for, was one having only one leg. This proved an advantage to the batsman rather than the opposite in that the leg was capable of emitting regular noises akin to a "snick". Any LBW appeal immediately became irrelevant the ball having touched "something" when the noise could mysteriously be reproduced at a second's notice and a "snick" to the wicketkeeper or first slip was followed by a waggle of the leg making "snicks" in all directions clearly indicating to one and all that the leg was up to its tricks again! Trouble was, he was a good bat and a very difficult man to remove.

We quickly came down to earth the following Sunday when we played one of our best fixtures of the year against Balliol College. In a way it enabled us to make comparisons — we were very much self-taught. I don't think we had television sets to enable us to watch first-class cricket, certainly there were no coaches, and this game was against mainly public school boys who had progressed to university. The batsmen defended their wickets — plenty of pad, confident, purposeful strokes, drives off the legs and the full treatment for any ball not on a length. Yes, it certainly was a yardstick, many of our opponents went on to achieve great things often to the detriment of their cricket. Richard Sharpe, the England stand-off (and he subsequently played for Cornwall CCC) was one, and Henry Brook, subsequently a cabinet minister. I shall always remember Tomkeys, one of the best bowlers I have ever seen, simply because he could bowl undetected cutters, going both ways off a faultless length. It wasn't even a case of reading him, he just did the business. I understand he subsequently ended up as a foreign attache giving up cricket at a relatively young age.

What I did not realise at the time was that one of the visitors would crop up repeatedly during coming years and that our paths would cross more than once. It was Jeff Stanyer, an off-spinner of great note, who subsequently played for Exeter CC and Devon Dumplings (their highest wicket taker of all time) and eventually became an author having written a tome on the History of the Exeter CC.

Players come and players go, and this season saw the moving on of "Whirlwind" Wheatley, who had given us the edge with his pacey opening bowling, and in a lesser team would certainly have batted higher. He played a classically straight bat, had a good range of scoring shots and a fair share of patience but he could be ruffled! It was at Filleigh that he was involved in one of the funniest incidents I have seen on a cricket field. Martin was batting about No.8 and was running out of partners when he was joined by Bill "Two-spin" Shortridge. Bill was in his usual attire with his white trousers, a trifle short and firmly held around his waist by a fireman's belt of brown polished leather, three to four inches thick. There was no question of a sweater and short sleeves were the order of the day. What Martin did not realise was that Bill was unwell and was approaching delirium. They quickly exchanged words and Martin made it quite clear to Bill that this was his day with the bat and he would take charge. Bill should give him the strike at every opportunity. Bill played the first ball into the covers and began running — the way he was facing! This happened to be to square leg and Bill set off, legs pumping (and by pumping I mean knees almost up to the chin!). Martin, meanwhile, had set off towards Bill's end, saw Bill running in an entirely different direction and having reached the half-way point, decided something was wrong and chose to return to the end from which he had come. At this point, Martin gave the clear command "Go back" but Bill was still running, knees to chin style with bat fully extended, and was probably thirty yards from the wicket. Martin's futile cry was changed to "Come back" but still Bill pounded on. Martin re-made his ground, but Bill charged on and into the pavilion probably thinking he had run a four. The amazing thing was that he had never left his crease and so there was never a question of being run out. Bill had a fever and promptly was obliged to retire leaving Martin stranded on a "not out" which he felt he could have improved upon had Bill not gone "walkies".

Later in the year, a compelling cricket character made his entrance onto the North Devon cricketing scene. Mike Jaquiss was a rapid bowler by any standards with a rather smooth chesty action. Regulatory batting gear usually comprised a box (usually by way of a plastic cup), gloves with rubber spikes and little else apart from the possibility of a towel being stuffed down one's trousers. This hardly seemed enough against Mr Jaquiss. Mike was quick! Our first encounter I well remember at Raleigh CC's ground at Barnstaple. On entering the pavilion there on the notice board was a handwritten letter signed by MJ inviting the players to come to catching practice. This was something unheard of even if it was at the suggestion of the captain let alone a new upstart. I went to the wicket, quickly lost my partner who had his stumps duly uprooted and was joined by Ken Harris, who kept goal for the same soccer side as I played in during the winter months. He had great difficulty in making out the wicketkeeper and slip cordon who could almost be regarded as boundary fielders. This called for an immediate discussion and decision as to tactics to be adopted in such an unusual situation. We quickly came to the conclusion that by simply dropping bat on ball and running regardless should result in at least six runs per over, there would be no one at the wicket to receive throw-ins so the chances of a run out were quite remote, the temperature would rise as the bowler grew more frustrated, and the wicketkeeper would be absolutely shattered. The ploy worked wonderfully well, forty more runs being added (mostly singles), for no wickets and we ended up with a good total to defend. The ploy also produced a considerable number of extras.

This brings me to another thought. The batsmen talked, exchanged ideas and views, and certainly discussed bowlers and the best way of playing them. This could not always be backed up by technique but at least there was application.

It was during this season that the club experimented with a Festival Week. It probably made sense insofar as instead of having midweek games and struggling to raise sides, many of the regular players took part of their annual holiday that week and so reasonably balanced sides could take the field. This was at a time when most had two weeks' holiday a year and overseas travel only occurred when there was a war!

One of our opponents was "Whiteway & Whimple CC", very much the creation of Richard Whiteway himself and as such new rules were often implemented to make the game more interesting. 'Awke always referred to the team as "Whimps" screeching out the name at a very high pitch and in time, the players all knew each other quite well and we had the most enjoyable games, both home and away.

Playing away was an experience bar none in that the pitch was at the front of RW's rather large house with a massive oak standing firm inside the boundary on the one side, and bounded by cider apple orchards on the other. The tree was a feature, certainly not to be felled, and so the simple alternative of painting a line on the trunk of the tree at head height solved the problem except for the unfortunate bowler hoping for a catch only to see the tree get in the way. Above the line — four, below the line — two. It was not unusual for W & W to "employ" workers who happened to have a bat or ball with them, and I well remember the many encounters with Smithy, who had played league cricket in the north, and could bowl the inswinger and outswinger to order — something almost unheard of in those days when new balls were at a premium.

We thought that RW was being over generous one day when I think we had the better of his team on the field but he kindly offered us the opportunity of taking home some of his windfalls from the adjoining orchard. Eating them was probably the quickest way of losing teeth and the after effects (hardly "after" — the effects were virtually immediate) were devastating but good for weight loss.

We often played twelve aside — if the match ended prematurely we played "NS" (non serious i.e. a scat match), and nearly everyone had a bat or bowl. Many of the spectators (and we very often had a full house in those days) much preferred the "scat match" thinking this to be the way serious cricket should be played.

Towards the end of the season, the rains would often come just that little bit early, moistening pitches and making the outfield grow just that little bit faster. And so it was at Barnstaple on the 16th August. The football season was just about to start and with the local football ground adjoining, rather loud music was played before, during and after that game. When a bowler talks about rhythm, he usually means a regular pace perhaps quickening a little at the end and this is difficult to accomplish with a noisy brass band giving its all. For this reason, there were times when playing at Barnstaple became unsettling and the four pace run up ended up with a twirl or two in time with the music and a complete lack of concentration.

We had only made a modest total but appreciated the conditions which were far from easy. The opposition found the conditions an absolute disaster with the ball turning at right angles and no batsman reaching double figures. Once the wickets began to fall, the field closed in as no way was the ball going to run to the boundary with the long grass. All was probably lost when BL came in. Not the happiest of men at any time, Bob could be a clean hitter and he was certainly stubborn, so we expected some resistance — no way would he roll over. Obviously he had thought about his ordeal and psyched himself up for combat. I think his first thought was to slow down proceedings, get us on edge, and to do this, he took guard and then proceeded to point his bat at every one in the field, one by one, as if to make a firm mental note. The wicketkeeper was even included (as if Bob and everyone else did not know where the wicketkeeper stood!). He finished off with the two short legs who were within inches of his waving bat. The whole procedure took what seemed to be five minutes or more — he might even have checked his guard with the umpire a few times, and then indicated that he was ready. A vicious spinner followed, Bob fended and the first ball lofted to forward short leg — the last man Bob had singled out for attention before inviting the bowler to bowl!

It was perhaps interesting to note that in a reasonable season where more matches were won than lost, runs per wicket for were 13.05 and against 12.24. How can this be reconciled with the present day.

The highlight of the 1959 season was the extension of the clubhouse to provide an outside wc. This was built with the aid of a grant from the Council but it saved both time and pain when one could use it immediately before batting, whereas walking along a main road one hundred yards or so to the public toilets was embarrassing and took an age when one had to pass along a line of spectators. In addition, the timing had to be perfect if a dropping down the order was to be averted. The £90 appeared to have been well spent.

The 21st June, 1959, was a day for me to remember for a number of reasons. Batting first against the local school Old Boys, Mervyn Bird scored one hundred and forty-four not out, a truly magnificent knock recorded by his wife on a newly acquired cine camera. The shots opened up with views of the ground, Mervyn walking to the wicket, a few seagulls and then the wife pressed the button just as Mervyn hit the ball. Instead of cricket and an innings of immense skill and power, we had what looked like a martial arts exhibition with ne'er a ball striking the boundary.

The printers at the local newspaper had decided to go on strike and so there was no edition to record this massive knock nor yet the bowling which followed.

Jared Collins was asked (for about the first time ever!) to bowl from the bottom end at Westward Ho! which meant bowling uphill. To the unthinking, bowling down a slope should allow most bowlers to bowl much more quickly but the ball tends to skid through without biting into the surface. The sea breeze also gusts from left to right taking the ball into the right-handed batsman. I suddenly found that bowling up the slope meant a cross wind which would drift the ball away from the right-hander and the ball would bite into the pitch and do its stuff. Having posted over two hundred runs, our opponents were very much at a disadvantage and after our pace bowlers had done their stuff, it was my turn to record a ten wicket haul for the first time. Luck always has to play its part as there are others trying at the other end. The umpire, an academic, helped no end by asking questions throughout — "What was that? What was the grip? Was that the cutter? Can you do it again?" I think there were times when we were playing our own little game and the batsmen (mostly his friends) were the victims. The real highlight, however, was the subsequent film show but there was no film left to record the bowling.

Shortly afterwards, we went back to Raleigh CC at Barnstaple — many of whose players became very well known to Andy Davies and myself as a result of tours to the Cheltenham area in later years and we often meet both at the ground and on the golf course. On this particular occasion, batting No.3 for Raleigh was a very promising young man who had just left school and had made quite a name for himself as a batter. What I did not know, however, was that before he came in to bat, he had a word with Henry Smale (who turned out to be Raleigh's top-scorer that day) and asked him how to play my off-breaks. This gave Henry an opportunity to expound all his theories, much to his delight. The batsman came in quite confident that plenty of bat and pad would keep out any tweaking ball on a fine Raleigh wicket and with one run to his name, faced the spinner with confidence. Two well pitched up balls — pace forward, plenty of pad, plenty of bat — no trouble. Ball number three was the "Miller Roundarm", delivered from the edge of the crease with round arm action, reasonably fast and hopefully cutting from leg to off. The batsman was still thinking about going forward, bat and pad, whilst his wicket behind him was shattered.

He stormed off, immediately sought out Henry and said "Why didn't you tell me about the quicker ball?"

"You didn't ask." Henry still tells the tale with gusto.

The season went on well into September with Mervyn Bird rounding off his fourth successive season by scoring over a thousand runs and Jared Collins took one hundred and fifty-four wickets, an improbable figure unlikely to be beaten having regard to the subsequent advent of league cricket and the restriction on the number of overs a bowler can bowl. 'Awke thought this unfair as if he was restricted when bowling, why couldn't batsmen be subjected to some similar restraint! He even suggested that batters be made to retire when they had scored twenty-five runs!

1960 — And so to another season. We were always wondering what new faces (hopefully attached to cricketing bodies) might appear and an initial club opening game was arranged to get rid of winter rust. My immediate reflection was that faster and faster bowlers were appearing calling for greater application and patience. Mike Jaquiss was strutting his stuff with Raleigh at this stage and Whipton turned up with Bert Smith. I well remember my first encounter with Bert and a straight forward defensive stroke reverberated up the arm and into the body. Thicker towels were called for to hitch into the jock strap hoping that this would, in some small measure, protect the thigh muscle. We knew, however, that in the case of Bert, a few turned down appeals (followed by the fastest deliveries of the day) would result in a slight strain and Bert would leave the field for the shelter of the wooden changing rooms. It did not always work but thank goodness Bert relied upon speed rather than guile which certainly must have taken it out of him. He did receive justified recognition and eventually played for the county.

Our matches with Bideford Nomads were always contested in the best of spirit, the majority of the players on the field having been Old Boys of Bideford Grammar School. As such we had great regard for each other but there was always plenty of banter. 'Awke used to marvel at the patience of Bob Harding, a fragile looking opening bat, who was always difficult to dislodge and loved his cricket so much. He had a ritual in that before playing each ball, he seemed to tap his heart with clenched fist just to make sure that he was still alive, and the right hand would then rejoin the bat ready for a deflection rather than a forced drive. Conservation of energy was a must. 'Awke would always be waiting for what he called "the pen and ink shot", a delicately played, lofted shot over however many slips the bowler would wish to muster. The ball would seemingly run down the length of the bat to be elevated over third man and thence race to the boundary. A rarely played shot, but one of great distinction only played by those 'Awke would designate as "masters".

Another batsman appearing on the scene that year was young Dave King of Barnstaple. Barnstaple were developing into a very useful side with some quality players. Dave did play a few seasons with Bideford and for technique and patience he must surely rank amongst one of the best and yet most modest batsmen in the county without ever receiving any form of recognition. One of his trade marks was to bat well back in the crease and he always watched the ball right onto the bat. He knew where he wanted the ball to go and if it did not go exactly where he wanted it to go, he regarded this as a bad shot. A good ball was kept out, the bad ball would receive the treatment — what could be simpler. Had he been so inclined, he could have gone so much further with a technique that ensured success on many a dicey wicket. When he did eventually join us, he was able to average sixty one season on

*"One of his trade marks was to bat well back
in the crease and he always watched the ball
right onto the bat"*

variable wickets with rarely a false shot.

My other memory of this player was when we played against Barnstaple and he led a brilliant rearguard action batting right through. He clearly felt that we had deserved a win and when we neared the time when stumps would be drawn, he merely walked down the wicket to a lofted spinner put his bat under his arm and kept walking. He had shown us that he was the master and that his side did not deserve a draw even if it was only a friendly. During his stay with us, I saw him take apart a Sussex professional with the greatest of ease, his stance position behind the crease giving him added time to play the away cutter which he did with great aplomb. A certainty for my Best XI.

It was interesting to see a report of the District Council at that time discussing the future of the cricket club and the ground at Westward Ho! We regularly attracted large crowds, cars parked along two sides of the ground and we knew of supporters from away who would request copies of the fixture list each year so as to plan their holidays to coincide with our Festival Week. Some councillors complained about the ground being used as an unofficial car park — "Were we not bothered about old cars dripping oil on to the square" — and this was followed by a suggestion that "It may be advantageous to the Council to do away with the cricket ground and use it as a car park". Thank goodness, the previous owners who sold the field to the Council did so with a covenant that the ground should always be used for recreational purposes, something the councillors should have been aware of. The review of the lease situation, however, always introduced some uncertainty playing havoc with the name of the club which had to be reviewed on a seven yearly basis as and when a new lease was under consideration. The name was the least of our considerations.

During the Festival Week there was a most interesting development which opened up a completely new interest for certain privileged members of the cricket club. A barbecue was held at the ground together with country dancing at which a select group of the cricketers provided the music. Tony Hudson played the piano but the backbone was provided by Roy Bird and Peter Williams, both of whom played for local bands on a semiprofessional basis. Peter was a drummer whilst Roy was a superb piano accordion player, who could also play the piano and seemingly get a tune from any form of instrument. Skiffle was "in" and for the moment Andy Davies played a tea chest by way of double bass, Pat Turner was no mean guitar player, and I adjusted to the washboard, a great favourite with Lonnie Donegan. We gradually modified and in addition to the washboard, I subsequently acquired a double bass and Peter, Roy, Pat and I played at quite a number of varied functions, many of which were, or became, hilarious. At times we were "booked" to play in village halls and at Christmas functions when the main local bands were not available, and with Roy and Peter we always managed to fulfil the booking, although there were a few close shaves.

A number of such events readily spring to mind. Roy played semiprofessional with Norman Cummings and his Orchestra, often backing the major bands in the country which appeared at The Queen's Hall, Barnstaple. This included Ted Heath, The Shadows and the like and so there was some quality there. I, in the meantime, was working for the local authority and had risen to the dizzy heights of junior committee clerk, involving me in evening meetings. One evening, Roy (he, like his brother Mervyn, was a bit of a joker) asked if I would play at The Alwington Parish Hall. I said I had a meeting but he said "Never mind, come out afterwards." At that time, I had the two stroke motor bike and a yellow flying suit which repelled all weathers (well, nearly) and this would enable me to dash straight from the Town Hall to Alwington for part of the session. As this was a "public appearance", I went along to the local ironmonger and bought a new washboard, and the needlework shop provided me with eight new thimbles.

Meeting over, I donned the flying suit and headed north-west to Alwington. On arrival, I was amazed by the sound and quality of noise emanating from the hall which was literally jumping with happy young bodies. I felt somewhat overdressed but on making my way into the hall I could see about half a dozen resplendent musicians on the stage complete with green jackets and red bow ties. Roy was on the accordion and Norman Cummings was playing the piano as usual in addition to leading the "orchestra". Norman motioned me towards a rather large folding wardrobe in which there was an array of green jackets, complete with bow ties, and suggested I should find one the right size, and take my place on stage. The empty seat was right at the front! The evening was going so well I might have got away with doing nothing at all but Norman motioned me to play (after about fifteen minutes soaking in the atmosphere) and I struck out, all eight fingers working in a frenzy to make an impression on the new board. I think I must have got somewhat carried away as the drummer gave me a nudge to have a rest, which I was very pleased to do. We got through the evening which was a new and thrilling experience for me but the drummer suggested that I might have a future elsewhere and offered to sell me a double bass (his brother being an expert player). I sensibly took the hint, saw the double bass and ignoring the woodworm I made him an offer he could not refuse.

At the time I gave little thought to any transport problem which might arise and my mode of transport had graduated to a Ford Anglia (the two door variety) but at least the double bass would lie across the front seat when pulled forward and project across the back. Anyone wishing to cadge a lift with me would have to sit in the front bent forward in the recovery position. I had to have the instrument restringed (frayed gut plays hell with the fingers), the woodwork treated and Roy kindly introduced me to a few "riffs". All of a sudden, I began to take notice of all the pop records of the time where the background beat played such a major part

*". . . all eight fingers working in a frenzy to make an
impression on the new board"*

and one riff could very easily be adapted in addition to which I would practise whilst playing hit records.

One evening, a knock came to the door — it was Roy. "Come with me, a minute." Out I went, he drove up the road a mile or two and we stopped at a house in a quiet lane on the outskirts of town, and adjoining the house was an original barn. We walked in, proceedings stopped, and the organiser announced "The orchestra has arrived." I just kept quiet having no idea what was happening or what I was supposed to do but it appeared that the husband and wife we had called on annually wrote a musical play to be performed in village halls over the Christmas period and had approached Roy about providing the music! "The orchestra has arrived" — this now took on a meaning. My highlights came when the leading man opened the wall safe to find that the jewels had been stolen and I had to make a thunderous noise on the double bass prior to the lights fading!

Peter Williams had been asked by his brother's employers to provide music for a Christmas works party at one of the major local hotels and as was usual at the time, he gathered together a few of his mates to perform for fun and enjoy a few beers. It all had to be done on a shoestring and so Roy, Peter and I agreed to do whatever was necessary to make the evening a success. We think that Peter had a somewhat more complicated involvement in that he also provided the other entertainment, a magician. The evening turned out to be quite hilarious once again and hardly likely to be repeated.

Having played for some dancing, we came to the cabaret. For this, the entire audience was shuffled up to one end of the room, the band stayed in a small recess at the side with the audience away to the right. The Great Mysto appeared dressed in top hat and tails — he was Peter's father-in-law and eighty if a day. His assistant was his wife (of similar age) dressed in short skirt and fishnet stockings. It spelt of disaster from the start. He took off his top hat, gave it to his assistant

"His assistant was his wife (of similar age) dressed in short skirt and fishnet stockings"

and peeled off his gloves throwing them one at a time into the hat (one missed). Making sure that the audience was well away to our right, he blindfolded his wife who was then facing us. There was one eyepiece missing, the one further away from the audience, but she was looking straight at the band. The Great Mysto then produced some very large playing cards, waved them in front of the audience and asked them to pick out one which they did, and he waved this around in the air making sure that his wife could have a good look with her "free" eye. She got two out of three right! This was not the end of it. The audience clapped, she turned and faced her audience to take a bow quite forgetting that she still had her blindfold on. It was an unbelievable performance. The next trick was an equal disaster, a member of the audience being asked to select a card from a "fixed" pack; the Great Mysto threw the cards into the air, stabbed at them with a sword to "spear" the selected card. The spring in the handle needed a little more oil, went about two inches, so that instead of the playing card being impaled at the end of the sword, it was right down the blade near the handle! It could only have come up!

They were very happy times — things did not appear quite so complicated and we laughed at ourselves.

1961 — With a sandy subsoil and the gentle sea breeze, the wicket at Westward Ho! always gave encouragement to the spin bowler, even more so when two spinners were able to work in tandem. 1961 saw the advent of Sam Whalley, a local tax inspector and very fine off-spin bowler, taking five wickets in each of his first two games. Unaware of his occupation, banter amongst the players as to whether one of them had any eggs for sale lifted the lid on a "black economy". The trembling tax evader was summoned to the tax office expecting a reprimand but he was asked if he could accommodate another customer!

During a lengthy period at Westward Ho! I have come across wicketkeepers who have varied in class and style.

Smithy was the first, a short man with a lump on the back of his neck, but someone who was a bundle of activity behind the stumps, keen to direct his bowler as regards line and length and a great encouragement to any younger player.

He was followed by Cliff Cudmore — a regular stopper who used his pads as much as his gloves, and was lost on some of the subtleties. He tried to get me to institute a form of sign language to reduce the number of extras but unless he was actually looking when the signal was given he either missed the ball or required me to give more than one signal often resulting in the batsman getting the message before either keeper or bowler!

Peter Williams stood in from time to time, unexpectedly good for a casual operator, a menace to batsmen with plenty of chat and niggles, and his gloves were never very far from the stumps.

Young Andy Davies then appeared. He had to start from scratch but was so anxious to succeed and steadily mastered the art. An even greater asset was his ultimate knowledge of all batsmen and after a few seasons, he knew the strengths and weaknesses of about 75% of the regulars who played against us and this was even more of an asset when he became captain and could set the field. As it was, together with hand signals, we set most of my fields without the batsmen knowing much about what was going on. It was in May of this year that Andy scored his first fifty, at Whimple. I was delighted to have been at the other end and enjoyed the moment as much as he.

Possibly the last was Mr Wadham, the bank manager. He usually played on Wednesdays, carried his kit in a banjo case — I never did find out if he was a musician. I rarely played midweek but on an occasion when I did and Mr Wadham was playing, I fielded at cover. It was always my ploy to stand a little out of range, move in quickly early on and fire a swift low return over the stumps. This was by way of a warning shot and during the course of a game could save twelve to twenty runs with the batsmen hopefully not wishing to take a chance. The ball came my way, I scooped it up and fired it in just over the bails. Mr Wadham was not used to such service, he tended to be leaning back rather than into the ball and the next thing he was flat on his back. I was pleased to get back to Saturdays!

What would probably not be understood in today's game was the fact that very few sides had a 2nd XI and colts cricket associated with clubs was unknown. Most schools played cricket but thereafter it was very much a case of "If you are big enough and good enough" you would find yourself in the 1st XI. The difficulty here, however, that for the most part there were "stars", batsmen used to batting high up in the order, and the regular bowlers straining to be let loose.

I well remember at or about this time, everyone batting in the Bideford side down to No.10 had scored eighty or over so that there was always the prospect of runs coming from somewhere, even if the upper batsmen had an off day. This was indeed comforting and to maintain interest throughout the team, Nos.1, 2, and 3 on a Sunday, often batted at 7, 8 and 9 on a Saturday.

One of these, of course, was 'Awke whose prowess with the bat was often overlooked though he rarely gave his wicket away. In the June away fixture at Braunton, after seeing half the side out for just over fifty, 'Awke added a fifty of his own. A powerful right-handed bat (as opposed to a left arm quick bowler) his trade mark was his defensive shot played off the back foot. The amazing thing was that this stroke was played with his back foot off the ground, bending his knee at right angles in Long John Silver style. This probably allowed him to jab down with the bat with no obstruction.

In this very same game, "Noddy" Easton played for the Saturday 1st XI, a relative newcomer who certainly qualified by way of his idiosyncrasies. His real name was Tony and he was one of the upholders of the law in what was a relatively quiet town. He was a classic traffic cop and many is the time that I have seen him directing traffic at the end of the famous old bridge when the lights failed. At times, one wondered if Tony had caused them to fail as he always seemed to have a pair of white gloves handy and he would take up his position in mid-four crossway and keep the traffic flowing at an alarming speed. He stood about six feet two inches in height, but probably would not have troubled the weighing machine much beyond eleven stones without boots. His fearlessness was his trademark and my initial memory of him at Braunton was in the changing room, Tony had stripped down to his Airtex vest revealing firm but narrow shoulders and he announced that the day that they armed the police was the day he would retire. He certainly earned the description of fearless.

At the time, I was employed by the local Council and at one of the meetings, alarm was expressed that someone allegedly was stealing items from the Council's tip and the borough surveyor was instructed to advise the police to round up the miscreants.

The borough surveyor instructed his clerk to do this and in no time, Tony was assigned to deal with the matter not knowing if it was a major gang of criminals from outside the area or yet a few local youths having a bit of fun. Tony was the man. In no time, he had made an arrest — the clerk who had telephoned the police who had gone along to the dump to get a pair of wheels to build himself a garden trolley! Tony would not let go — this was another major arrest which had necessitated him going undercover. The miscreant did eventually get off (much to Tony's annoyance) but the clerk used to look out onto the bridge and felt he was getting his own back by naming Tony "Noddy". Tony's lithe, narrow figure hardly seemed burly enough to be atopped by his helmet and as he walked, his head went forward and backward on a lean neck, rather like the little dogs that present day car owners have in their back windows. Noddy did not appear to take exception and the name certainly stuck.

He was good fun to have around and a perfect foil for

'Awke. At the beginning of each season, he turned up with some new piece of equipment he had made — special batting gloves with extra padding, pads ditto, and his cricket bag always carried a pack of cards. No one ever played with Noddy as whenever it rained, he got out the cards and proceeded to shuffle them with one hand!

His bowling was steady medium pace and it was quite an experience fielding in close when he was bowling as the eyes had to be very firmly fixed on the batsman but no worries, Noddy's approach to the wicket, with his rather large feet, was reminiscent of a herd of buffaloes and there was no doubting when Noddy was on his way. Batting wise, he did progress to opening on occasion and I well remember when playing against The Cornish Choughs, he came up against a former England trialist in the pace department and was struck on the pad. Noddy had to come off injured, his reinforced padding not getting the seal of approval.

His fearless side came out on a number of occasions when he chose to field at short leg. Very often when we batted first and thought the pitch might offer some assistance to the spin bowlers when the visitors came to bat, the procession of players from the pavilion after tea became something of a forced march, as first in position got the job. Two or three made for the short leg positions and apart from one who had probably the quickest reactions I have ever come across, the remainder were much of a muchness and so it was with Noddy. One should not decry keenness.

One such game was against Combe, but their quickie had dug an appreciable pit at the top end and in those days, little was done to reinstate the damaged foot holes during the tea interval. We had scored a testing number of runs and so immediately went into the attack with Noddy ensconced at forward short leg. At the ready, Noddy resembled something akin to a bent pin (from the bowler's end) and our quickie steamed in, his foot landed on the side of the pit dug by the Combe paceman and the ball hurtled out of control, well down the leg side. There was little time in which to warn Noddy, the ball may be said to have struck the bull's-eye and one wondered if the umpire's cry of "No ball" needed an explanation or possibly a search party! On another occasion, Noddy took a nasty dap on the head resulting in vertigo, but that is another story. It was always good to have him in the side.

Towards the end of the season we played one of our rare games away, this time traversing the border into Cornwall for a match against Bude. The pitch seemed to be on a cliff edge, exposed to the sea and elements on one side, with an assured gusting breeze. On this occasion we lost, mainly due to a splendid knock by a young man wearing a jazz hat, and very thick glasses. His defence was good, he annoyingly played many a shot to leg which seemed destined for elsewhere, and whilst a bowler felt that he was always in with a chance against an uncertain (apparently trembling) batsman, before you knew where you were, he had a very good score against you. It was my privilege to play for and against Nick B on quite a number of occasions and he undoubtedly was one of the most talented all-round sportsman one could wish to meet — he was also one of the best "gamesmen"! Our paths were to meet many times, particularly on cricket tours.

1962 — As usual, almost the first report of the season related to the AGM and a proposition that the annual subscription should be raised. This should be justified and one player suggested that if subscriptions increased, parking spaces should be reserved for the players. Though the memory tends to dim, this clearly indicates that at that time matches at Westward Ho! were a considerable attraction. Gates for the previous year (a green box taken around the ground and shaken in front of spectators) produced £195, exactly twice the amount received by way of subscriptions. There was car parking along two sides of the ground, a top fence (adjoining the main through road) for spectators to lean on and a limited amount of seating on the western side where the wooden shed doubling as changing rooms stood. A team sheet listing the names of those taking part would be displayed on a notice board in the main High Street in Bideford and it was always embarrassing to be looking at this and hearing someone behind saying "Oh, Robbie's not playing, not worth going to!" We had plenty of other very good players but Robbie was always a law unto himself and produced the unexpected more often than not. Travelling expenses had shot up from £11 to £29 for the season.

At this time, the Hatherleigh Cricket Club was not on our fixture list though over the years many members of both clubs have become firm friends. The club is now well established with an attractive ground just off the roundabout at the Okehampton approach to the town. It is level, has a second pitch for the youngsters adjoining, and the clubhouse is a splendid asset. One thing which always impresses me is that one of the youngsters in the home side is given the task of thanking the tea ladies for a splendid meal between innings. The whole ground has an air of being well looked after — there are even attractive flowerbeds which never appear neglected.

Brian Jones and Charles Inniss remain my very good friends to this day and were always fun to play with or against. Brian was a patient and thoughtful opening batsman who would carve out runs with delicate strokes here and there without ever giving the bowler a hint that he might give his wicket away. Charles was (and is) an astute captain, organiser and tactician with the same approach to batting as Brian but coupled this with well flighted deliveries when called upon to bowl. Such players never surrendered and played the game in exactly the right spirit.

At the time, Hatherleigh was blessed with a couple of good opening bowlers. Well, actually, it was not just at that time, they seemed to go on for ever, rather like an institution. They were Rex B and Roy L. Roy was always there or thereabouts and the perfect foil for Rex who was a "Gough-like" creature, sturdily built, with a splendid whippy action and certainly no duffer with a bat.

Many of the Hatherleigh lads had been to Shebbear College, a fine educational establishment which seemed to host the sons of most farmers in North Devon and where a considerable amount of the time was spent on the playing fields. Farmers' sons seemed to have the right build for physical sports and the college had enthusiastic sports masters. Brian and Charles were Shebbear College products and worthy ambassadors.

I had the feeling that Rex had learnt his cricket elsewhere and for a great many years could always be relied upon to provide the backbone with both bat and ball in addition to being a must for any local representative side. Roy always hung in there, keeping things quiet at the other end, and picking off batsmen who were prepared to give a chance (and there were many).

Charles was able to tell me a splendid tale of the duo who enjoyed many joint successes both at home and away. Playing away (well away up on Exmoor I am told), they skittled the home side leaving Hatherleigh the proud winners of a lustily fought battle against considerable odds. Few clubs had bars, therefore Rex and Roy celebrated in dramatic style at the local hostelry, steadily replacing lost fluid (and more) with a special brew favoured in those parts. The night went well, the match was played and replayed, with Rex and Roy bowling faster and faster each time. Mine host called "Time" and the jubilant Hatherleigh team was rounded up and hustled onto the charabanc for the long journey home. They had not got far when Rex and Roy called for the bus to stop. After all, they had lost more fluid than most and this had had to be replaced whatever the consequences. The bus halted in a small country lay-by and Rex and Roy raced towards the back of the lay-by looking for a sheltered spot to relieve themselves. The ground seemed to be moving (some beers have this effect) and one of our triumphant opening bowlers (I know not which) fell over a hedge and landed in the middle of a man's naked back. The tale is that a little female voice from below whispered "Thank you", with a sigh! If only I knew whether Rex or Roy was involved, I could verify the story!

Across the river from Bideford, the revival of the North Devon CC as a major force once again was about to take place. Always able to attract fine players coming into the area due to the splendid setting and quality of the ground, some home-grown young men were just about to make the grade and take the game to the opposition. Many years before, the Molland brothers could always be relied upon to make runs and take wickets and this seemed to be a repeat performance with David and Bill Shepherd. David was an outstanding batsman, solid of frame, but with all the time in the world to play shots all round the wicket and demolish attacks. Bill was a very fine left arm spinner who bowled the "Chinaman", in addition to being a quality batsman although not perhaps in the class of his elder brother. Both played for the county and David represented the Minor Counties against most foreign tourists prior to playing as a professional county cricketer in the West Country. David subsequently became an international cricket umpire of the highest standard and is a world class figure in the cricketing world. It was wonderful to be in at the beginning of his remarkable career.

Perhaps one felt that standards were being set in North Devon when once upon a time, a county XI would rarely include anyone from that part of the county. As such, it may be said that many a fine cricketer from the north eluded the county net until the advent of David Shepherd.

In recent years, at a local level, I have not seen anyone attempt the "Chinaman". Bill was a prolific natural left-hander, getting plenty of turn probably due in no small measure to a stint on the Lords Groundstaff, but the wrist spinning "Chinaman" turned even more. In a way, there was no guile as with the right-hander's googly where one might think the ball was going to spin one way and then went the other — the "Chinaman" is there for all to see, that is, if you know what you are looking for. We had one batsman, who regularly scored runs, but when facing Bill he was like a rabbit in headlights, and the "Chinaman" would get him every time. I also saw this when I toured with Bill and we bowled together on a turning Gloucester wicket. So many padded up and seemed to be hit every other ball by the one that went the other way. It is almost too late when one has to face such a bowler — you need to be thinking about what to expect and then have some sort of plan to counteract it. Our batsman simply became a "rabbit".

After one Saturday game at Westward Ho! it was suggested that we should go back to the local hostelry, run by one of our players, and have a musical evening. It seemed a very good idea at the time and soon we assembled the orchestra which comprised Roy Bird on the piano, Peter Williams on drums, JC on bass and Pat Turner on guitar. I had never played in a pub before but in no time at all the music was flowing as was the beer, and it seemed that every time we played a request (and had a jolly good singsong), a round of drinks would follow. It was a splendid evening and going extremely well, until the local doctor (known as "The Leader" because he was difficult not to follow) suggested that when the pub closed, it would be an ideal night to go fishing.

We carried on playing, the temperature rose and the room became more crowded and in the end, it became quite a rave. Pat had one or two party pieces and was always anxious to play these but in the meantime strummed along lightly and any wrong notes were obscured by the semi-drunken singing. Watching Pat, however, was quite an experience in that he seemed to snap guitar strings with great regularity. He would wait until the end of a number, take off the broken string and hurl it behind the piano, rethread and away he would go again.

The landlord (Mervyn Bird) eventually called "Time" and it was almost a strange feeling coming back down to earth and whilst we were sitting quietly, The Leader appeared and announced that the timing was perfect and the fish were waiting to be caught. Like fools, we herded into cars and went to the cricket ground which is alongside the beach. We changed into bathing gear in the darkened cricket pavilion — there were no lights — and The Leader explained the tactics. Pat had a net (he said nothing about not having checked it!) and The Leader suggested that we walk about a mile or so down the beach towards the estuary and when we came to a suitable spot, he would give the command, and we would spring into action. The idea was that someone would take the end of the net and go out into the surf as far as he could and there would be additional fishermen at various stages in the water with The Leader on shore securing that end of the net. We would "process" (what a splendid word, and utterly appropriate) back towards the slipway simply engulfing the fish into the net, the two ends would be drawn together, and we would extract the fish which would be ideal for an early morning breakfast at a beachside cafe owned by a friend who would be woken up by The Leader to take part in our celebratory breakfast. At this stage, we gave little thought to the Sunday cricket match!

I, like the others, fell under the spell of The Leader to the extent that I ended up at the furthest point out in the surf with the end of the net. I had not really reckoned on the full impact of this important assignment. At best the surf was chest high and I had to keep the net taut, but there was a breaking surf so that every few seconds I seemed to be immersed completely. A fair amount of sea water was imbibed which did not exactly blend well with the splendid ale offered at the Northam Inn but I continued to be inspired by The Leader who cajoled his troops from the sandy beach. It was like plodding through treacle, arms high, waves breaking, stars shining above and then the order came to draw the two ends of the net together carefully entrapping the fish. This was done, not entirely successfully, as it was

*"At best the surf was chest high and
I had to keep the net taut . . ."*

so easy to fall over in the dark and when the team finally assembled on the shore, we quickly realised that we had been outdone by the fish. We had caught nothing.

The Leader quickly inspired us once again by suggesting that our inexperience had let us down and by not staying on our feet the entire time, we had allowed the fish to wriggle free over/under the net whilst we were recovering. We were (he told us) mastering the art and the next time should really reap dividends. I found myself as outrider once again amid the translucent waves which were not getting any smaller, but at least we were slightly under a mile from our destination having covered almost one hundred yards. Under inspired leadership, we plunged on, repeated the intricate procedure and, once again, no fish. Pat decided it was about time we had a look at the net. It was full of holes — no matter how we improved our technique, we did not have the equipment and were destined to fail. In addition, it was getting colder, we had been in the water a long time, and the sea water/ alcohol combination was beginning to ferment.

In orderly fashion, following our masterly Leader, we dragged the net back to the cricket field, used the car headlights to see into the pavilion which enabled us to find our clothes. I attempted to dress, I was cold, felt far from well and the last thing I remember was being violently sick. In the dim background I heard someone say "God, all over Raymond's pads." I was past caring, somehow got to bed, only to find that the pillow continued to emulate the movement of the sea and waves with the ceiling constantly coming and going.

Needless to say, one of the players cried off the next day, I had visions of our skipper going out to bat with bits of tomato on his pads and was in fear that I would be drummed out. It is an awful thought, but good friends turned up early next morning, did a good cleaning up job and the skipper made runs as usual. There must be a moral here somewhere — always beware of a born leader and certainly do not mix alcohol with sea water!

I have mentioned elsewhere that there was something of a barrier between North and South Devon and it was only on the rare occasion that a South Devon side would agree to send a full strength side to the north. The introduction of league cricket somewhat overcame this anomaly though it was not such an attractive proposition when you were in a team which had to motor down to Torquay about five times a season and to Exeter or Plymouth for the remainder of the Saturday matches.

It was in September of this season that Barton Torquay sent up quite a strong side, including the professional Jack Kelly, and a couple of other county players, but the home team stood its ground and the spinners once again wrapped up a good win.

1963 — One of the reasons for writing this tome is to record an era when cricket was very much a fun game with a serious element — the natural desire to win. As a club, the past is very much unwritten and from time to time snippets appear indicating that cricket at Bideford and Westward Ho! goes back a great many years with hardly a mention. At one time I came into possession of a fixture card for the Northam Cricket Club and Westward Ho! Cricket Club dated 1902. On the cover the officers were listed with Rev. Preb. M. D. Dimond-Churchward as president, Rev. J. B. Grimes, the treasurer and secretary of the Northam Club whereas Rev. F. I. Anderson was the secretary of Westward Ho! in addition to being captain. One had the feeling that perhaps the Lord was on their side! Bishops Tawton (about eleven miles) was the farthest away fixture and one could almost envisage a couple of horses with carts being enlisted to take the team and kit away, probably leaving the night before. Club colours were expected to be worn in all practice games and matches, with caps available from the respective secretaries. Matches were played on the Burrows (the outreaches of the Royal North Devon Golf Club), in addition to Westward Ho! itself, which was the home of the United Services College.

Inside the fixture card I found a discoloured cutting relating to a match between Appledore and Northam played on the Burrows which resulted in a dramatic win for Northam by fifteen runs. Appledore mustered forty-nine runs whereas Northam amassed sixty-four. Four batsmen got into double figures, two a side, whereas the bowlers had a field day.

My reason for mentioning this is that a scrapbook relating to the 1963 season opens up with an extract from The West Buckland School Magazine which "looked back" and found that in 1888, the first century ever made against the school's cricket XI was by the Rev. W. R. W. S. Vida, playing for Bideford Cricket Club. The club and ground obviously hold many secrets about its early formation and subsequent history which probably now will have been lost forever. This is such a pity.

Probably what has not helped is the number of times the club was obliged to change its name. I truly believe that I joined the Bideford Cricket Club which played at Westward Ho! We enjoyed a reasonably good relationship with our landlords, the Northam Urban District Council which administered Northam, Westward Ho! and Appledore. We had a relatively simple lease which had to be renewed every seven years which gave the Council the opportunity of reconsidering the terms of our letting and with a new Council membership, this inevitably gave rise to a discussion on the name of our club. Bideford became "Bideford & District CC" which adequately would include Northam, Westward Ho! and Appledore. Seven more years elapsed, there was a further review and the Council suggested that we should change the name to Westward Ho! and District CC, as we played at Westward Ho! To cap it all, there was an amalgamation in 1970 of the Bideford and Littleham Cricket Clubs and to satisfy EVERYONE the name became The Bideford, Littleham and Westward Ho! Cricket Club!

The season saw one or two promising young players appear on the scene including Geoff Folland, a star performer with Shebbear College, who was one of those enviable young men whose athletic frame and balance allowed them to play most games with élan. A fine batsman, he scored his first fifty for the club in early May and followed this with a century shortly afterwards. In the field he was certainly no slouch and his medium paced deliveries always provided a useful alternative to the now ageing opening bowlers who were beginning to suggest that guile was more important than speed! He went on to star for the local rugby club where he excelled in all positions outside the scrum. I also remember a challenge sports evening involving the local soccer club and he scored a hat-trick when playing soccer against the home club, and he is still one of the best table tennis players in the league after forty years or so. Being a farmer must have helped, Geoff always seeming to be in the peak of health apart from the inevitable hair loss.

One thing I shall always remember about Geoff was an innings which he played at Instow against Mike Jaquiss, when the latter transferred his allegiances from Raleigh to North Devon. It wasn't really an innings and Geoff certainly did not play! The older members of the team suggested that playing an extra pacey bowler might call for a slightly different technique, certainly in the initial stages. We thought Geoff had taken this on board but in no time at all he was back in the pavilion having been bowled while still performing his backlift! Mike was quick.

Meanwhile, nearby North Devon CC was certainly on the up with David Shepherd bolstering the batting, and in August we were hammered (actually it was a draw, but Bideford contributed little) by a side featuring three Devon county players, a former Essex II, and a Norfolk county bowler.

It was on occasion that Bideford were confronted by good teams of this ilk and then the chips were certainly down and it needed a very good side with all top players performing. I always felt the Bideford v North Devon fixture was a case of "men" against "boys" with the better players clearly enjoying the encounter but it was no place for the faint hearted. A good performance in such a fixture was a performance to be savoured.

It was easy to feel envious of the players in the better sides who obviously had been to schools where cricket was encouraged and knowledgeable coaching took place. In this respect, we, at Westward Ho!, were indeed fortunate to have such teams as Denstone Wanderers visit us for many years; "The Hares", doctors from St Mary's Hospital the majority of whom were university lads who had come up through public schools, and the likes of Balliol College brimming with young men who played "straight" and could punch a spinner through mid-wicket with the greatest of ease. With many local sides, getting rid of the first four or five exposed the "rabbits" and apart from the lusty slog or two, usually rashness set in after one or two "dot" balls and a bowler could be in business. Equally so, a good performance against these better sides had to be earned and the challenge was always there.

Bowling performances at the end of a season could become somewhat distorted when overnight moisture often affected the wicket and at times made the outfield slow. The members of Whimple & Whiteways CC were always game for a visit to Westward Ho! and could be relied upon to produce a team at the last minute to squeeze just another match into any season. And so it was this year and whilst the home side (with batting line up strengthened by the Shepherd brothers of Instow and North Devon) found runs extremely easy to come by, the visitors found themselves very much on the losing end. The "Whimps" opening bat scored all twenty-four runs in the opening partnership and then a well-known local spinner took ten wickets for nine runs. Sadly he did not take the first wicket, otherwise it could possibly have been a record breaking eleven wickets in an innings, probably something unheard of outside the "Whimps v Bideford Series", but at least he bagged the last ten in succession, making it extremely easy for the scorer!

'Awke closed one of our seasons at or around this time by giving his own summation of Mike Jaquiss and his speedy deliveries at the club's annual dinner. Batting at No.8, 'Awke went in to face Mike, bowling at Instow from the seaward end from a point a few yards inside the boundary. He hurtled up to the wicket, the arm came over rather fast and 'Awke recounts "I didn't see anything. I didn't move. I just stood there." Mike was none too pleased and added a few paces to his already lengthy run. His next approach to the wicket was somewhat faster, 'Awke didn't see anything. He didn't move. He just stood there! The third delivery began from a launch pad on the boundary, knees were pumping, there was a gathering of speed, a high immaculate delivery but the effort was too intense and umpire Cecil Bird shouted "No ball" as Mike stepped over the front crease. A satisfied 'Awke announced to one and all — "I knew there was no ball!"

1964 — The season began on a political note, the Council suggesting that the club should change its name to Westward Ho! CC and the club resisting. A fiery Council meeting referred the matter to committee when one councillor asked what would happen if the club did not agree to change its name!

It was also a time when the club made a positive effort to recruit and encourage young players and The George Keen Trophy was presented to the club by scorer Miss Lil Keen, in memory of her late father, to be awarded annually to "The Best Young Player of the Season".

The attitude of the local authority towards the use of the cricket ground by the cricket club was somewhat motivated by a possible desire to incorporate the cricket ground in improving the holiday attractions of the resort. Whilst one could sympathise with such a sentiment, it was always felt that such forward thinking should not be at the expense of the cricket club which in itself was an attraction, at the time drawing large crowds, particularly on Sundays, and many visitors made a point of coming to Westward Ho! specially for the Cricket Festival Week, either as spectators or bringing along their kit in case the home side was short at any time. Some very strange names have appeared in our line-up during that week.

My involvement at that time was as secretary to the club but subsequently I have been involved with some very special people who deserve credit for preserving a great piece of local history and genuine feeling some people in the past had for the game. Here I must rely upon a few reports and an ageing memory.

I gather that in the very early days (at the turn of the last century) Westward Ho! was the home of The United Services College, located off what is now known as Atlantic Way, with playing fields stretching down to the pebble ridge which formed a barrier keeping out the raging Atlantic. The college was founded in September 1874 and Rudyard Kipling was one of the former pupils some of whose best known books bear witness to the education which he received at the college. The college closed down in March 1904. I am informed that three of the parents of students at the college decided that perhaps they should purchase what is now the cricket ground so that their sons, after leaving the college, could play cricket there as and when they wanted. I was subsequently able to confirm that one of the fathers had in fact captained the county side and obviously was keen to give his son every encouragement. One wonders if one could see this happening today. Such an arrangement would one day reach the end of its useful life, and so it was in 1936 when the field was conveyed to the local authority. It is here that I am searching deeply into my memory, but I recall that the price was the same as the three kindly gentlemen had paid when they purchased from the college — profit was not a motive only the encouragement to their respective sons to pursue their interest in cricket. There is something very gallant about this. The fathers had formed themselves into "The Westward Ho! Cricket Field Co. Ltd." and as such conveyed "The Cricket Field" to the Council with a restrictive covenant that *"the land was to be forever kept and used for purposes of recreation only and that no buildings other than those normally associated with recreation should be erected thereon"*. The future use of the field was, to a certain extent, preserved by the foresight of three very wise Victorian gentlemen though problems could arise as regards enforcement of the covenant. What would happen if no cricket club wanted to use the ground, and how would one interpret "buildings associated with recreation"?

One of the joys of having been associated with the club over a great number of years is that I have met some members of the families initially involved with the college and the ground, and the desire is still very much there to preserve the honour and traditions of the past. I sincerely hope that this will be the case — but what a wonderful story. Each time I have taken the field at Westward Ho! at the beginning of a match, my eyes cannot help but gaze at the former college, the outline remains the same with the headmaster's cottage at the side, but the main building has been converted into permanent flats which at least has preserved the outline and ensured the continued maintenance of a very important part of history. I also wonder whether Rudyard bowled "from the top end" or perhaps "up the hill". No other ground can have this feeling and it is no wonder that so many touring sides relish the idea of playing so near the sea in such a wonderful spot.

Because of the attraction of the ground, most of our away matches were played in May and then we could sit back and await the visit of teams to Westward Ho! Bude was usually one of our early away trips, a pleasant little jaunt down the coast, and a cliff top location constantly attracting gusty sea breezes. The sandy subsoil to the wicket area made it an attractive proposition for spin bowlers and the lofted delivery could waver in trajectory if the wind arrived at the right time.

We managed to pull off a victory on this occasion but the match was memorable for one particular dismissal — the running out of John Cork. Not a regular, and batting at No.10 (but one place above 'Awke), he took a time to settle but when the time came, he confidently struck the ball towards the boundary, ran safely to the opposing end making the fatal mistake of taking his eye off the ball. So confident was he that his strike was masterly, having downed his bat at the end of the first run he called for a second not realising that the ball was already in the bowler's hands. This was suicide of "kamikaze pilot" proportions and John was run out, but being John, it was regarded as just another hilarious incident to be recorded in a tome such as this.

In June, we welcomed another "star" who was to have a considerable impact on younger players in North Devon. Quite a number of years earlier, the whisper went around that there was an Essex CCC opening bat at RAF Chivenor, doing his National Service, and appearing in representative sides. He so liked the area that after National Service he took a teacher training course at St Luke's College, Exeter, but with contacts in North Devon, he was happy to play for us. I well remember his first knock. I had not seen batsmen wear inner gloves, he seemed to have far better pads that the rest of us and he certainly looked the part beneath a dark blue cap with Essex badge clearly indicating to bowlers that they were shortly to be in some trouble.

Raleigh could not have seen this in that their left arm spinner dropped a ball well up on Les's front foot and the ball rocketed to square leg at the speed of light only for KK to fail to get out of the way, somehow the ball striking his person and lodging itself somewhere. Ken, grasping what he thought was a heart attack, got his name into the score book as the catcher and goodbye LS and cap.

We did not have to wait long to see the real thing and Les Savill thereafter consistently took the bowling apart giving the bad ball what it deserved with an unexpected amount of power whilst the good ball was suitably acknowledged. Les was a particularly good coach, quick to spot weaknesses and it was this aspect of his interest in cricket that I felt was his greatest contribution. He did play for Devon but at the time was anxious to prepare a new career for himself firstly in teaching and thereafter in social work. He gave us something to aim at.

The day following his debut, Les played against Balliol College, Oxford, always one of the best cricketing sides we would come across in a season. Les made a splendid forty-six runs against a quality attack but we were able to declare with one hundred and seventy-one on the board. On paper Balliol had a good batting side, including one Tasmanian player, but they ended up forty runs short, Bideford spinners accounting for nine of the ten wickets which fell. I had six wickets for twenty-six runs in eighteen overs. I say this because I regarded this as one of my best performances ever having clean bowled five with turning off-breaks and having the sixth caught. As soon as the match was over, some of the Balliol players went back to the square to see if they could turn the ball on that wicket, and they could not. If only the magic had stayed!

The season was continuing to go apace with skipper Sam Whalley performing extremely well with his middle order batting and quality flighted off-spinners. His tactics were simple — bat first and then, having chosen himself and one other spinner at selection, would say: how many overs shall we give the quickies before we come on? Decisions based on such confidence are often successful.

It was in July that I received an unexpected invite — to play for Devon CCC against The Royal Navy at Plymouth. Les Savill was also in the side and the brothers David and Bill Shepherd of North Devon would also be there giving North Devon its greatest recognition for many, many years. I had previously played for a Devon Club & Ground XI ten years earlier, not being called upon to bowl in my final representative game that year due to a very wet pitch, and seemingly forgotten during which time I had chalked up over a thousand wickets for my club. This opened up a new facet of my cricketing life which I will continue elsewhere. I did, however, deem it a very great honour but felt, in some way, that I was being dished up as fodder for The Royal Navy. In case I forget later, I did take five wickets in the two innings which hopefully justified my selection.

In August we did agree to change our name — to Bideford & Westward Ho! CC. The Council was delighted!

Mid-August brought the Cornish Crusaders to Westward Ho! They were particularly strong this year and their No.3 scored a century without too much trouble enabling the visitors to declare with a very respectable total. What we hadn't expected was a visit by David Halfyard, a former Kent CCC professional, one of the best seam bowlers in the country until a motorbike accident cut his first-class career short, but hastened him to the west. He was still bowling seamers at this time, not particularly fast, though the faster ball appeared occasionally when a batsman annoyed him. The overall control and movement was that of a master.

Despite his injuries, David was still able to play in the Minor Counties for Cornwall and in one memorable match, virtually unlikely to be repeated, he took all ten wickets in the first innings and the first six in the next until rain stopped play. He was on for all twenty wickets in a match until deprived by the weather. This would not have been repeated, although we shall never forget Laker getting nineteen wickets against the Australians.

David subsequently came to live between Westward Ho! and Northam, just over a mile from the Westward Ho! Cricket Ground, but he still yearned for good cricket. His greatest attribute as a bowler was that he always wanted to get wickets (not a bad ambition for any bowler) and towards his latter years, he was still playing good quality Devon League cricket, slowing down another notch to bowl leg-breaks and googlies. His googly was not so easy to spot from the crease as it was from the fence and whilst I kept saying to myself "That is the googly" — the batsmen were not that sure and to the very end he was getting wickets.

He was an interesting man to talk to and a quality groundsman so that if we had a problem we would often consult him regarding the condition of our seaside wicket. I well remember spending a half hour or so with him at Westward Ho! watching a game and asking him about wicketkeepers. Having played for Kent, he had had first-hand experience of some of the greatest wicketkeepers of all time and he quickly gave Godfrey Evans top billing with Alan Knott close behind. I had seen Evans keeping to Doug Wright, allegedly a leg-spinner with googly, but to the unknowing he could well be taken as an opening bowler he was that fast. His third selection somewhat amazed me. It was Jesse Lawry who played for Cornwall. Jesse was small and neat, as tidy as they come. When he first played with David Halfyard for the county, he asked if David would spend some time with him in the nets in an attempt to understand what was going on. This to me was a measure of both men, the master and the one willing to learn. Thereafter they performed in perfect harmony and I have no doubt that Jesse played an instrumental part in those sixteen wickets in that fateful match in Cornwall which might have made cricketing history.

I well remember my first match for Devon — I asked the keeper if he wanted to know what I bowled. He suggested that I should keep aiming at his gloves! The "master" prepares before the performance!

1965 — "Some of our players are leaving and we all are growing older" was the announcement I made as club secretary at the AGM for the year. It is the fear of any reasonable side that growing old together will inevitably end in disaster unless there can be a steady influx which is extremely difficult when you only have a 1st team. Of necessity there has to be some form of rotation but the stronger players are needed to provide the backbone.

We welcomed two new players for the season one of whom was Roy Watson, a batsman from Weston-Super-Mare. I particularly mention this as having played a few seasons with Roy, he eventually departed the South West and I heard nothing more, that is, until I met him in 2001 at a Rotary National Conference where he was serving as a district governor for District 1040, West Yorkshire. It certainly is a small world.

Another new name appeared early in May, that of Mike Sparrey. I found him to be an extraordinary cricketer, seemingly with no cricketing background, but he was solidly built, powerful and with lightning reactions. He kept goal at soccer, with no great height and possibly a trifle overweight but again his reactions were extremely quick and he performed at a very good level. He also was an off-spinner, prone to rather more flight than myself, and preferred to bowl uphill (as any sensible bowler would) floating the ball away with the ever present sea breeze and biting into the slope which added to the turn. In the slips he was magic, a flashing hand and the ball was his. He batted left-handed, with considerable power, and a full toss would certainly be lifted back over the bowler's head for six, often a prodigious stroke with no doubt as to the ball's ultimate destination. His figures spoke for themselves as not only did he take over one hundred wickets one year but he also scored a thousand runs. Later he played for the county over 50s, alas for a short period only as he died at a relatively young age. Something that perhaps was to be expected having had a heart attack during his goalkeeping days. A most impressive, physical power player who could win matches virtually on his own.

Reading through old press reports is quite thought provoking and it confirms that with age the mind withers. Things you think you have remembered seemed not to have happened at all and many hair-raising performances have been totally forgotten. A headline in the local press in July recalled that Peter Williams, at forward short leg, took twelve catches in four games. The article stated *"Peter's favourite perch is at forward short leg, a position demanding implicit faith in the bowler and not a little courage, particularly when the batsman's eyes start to light up"*.

As a bowler, it makes the world of a difference having someone who will field in close and concentrate, but quick reactions are also a must. I find that this is something lacking today and certainly the younger players (probably the ones with the quickest reactions) are not permitted to stand close. I also suspect that the wickets are better, but forcing a batsman to play late to a turning "popper" is manna for someone with an extra sharp pair of hands who is prepared to concentrate. Twelve catches in a season is not bad — in four games it was phenomenal.

The local press were also pleased to announce that a garage in the area would be giving a barrel of beer to the batsman with the highest score during the month of July and also the person with the most meritorious bowling performances. What on earth do you do with a barrel of beer? Have it delivered to a pub and give your mates a good night out! Taking over fifty wickets in July directed the barrel of beer in the direction of Westward Ho! and a good time was had by all.

The beer must have had something to do with an exceptional yet annoying performance against Exeter Sunday Stragglers a short time afterwards. The local club having more than held their own against visiting and local clubs alike had the greatest possible difficulty at that time in obtaining 1st team fixtures, though "more senior" teams would visit them under abstruse names. So it was with Exeter Sunday Stragglers. At the time, the local club probably warranted a 1st XI game and would have fielded a full strength side but more often than not, the visiting club's name would be altered slightly — "Plymouth Queries", "Exeter Sunday Stragglers" — but in fact, quite often it was a good 2nd team with a sprinkling of 1st team players.

Against Exeter Sunday Stragglers, young Geoff Folland hammered one hundred and twenty-two out of one hundred and seventy-nine runs for the loss of five wickets declared, and the visitors were bowled out for eighty-four, the home spinner taking six wickets for one run. Perhaps the formation of leagues would eliminate such anomalies. The real test came a few days later when the club succumbed to North Devon once again, their star studded side having too many big guns, with county players performing well.

One of our favourite visiting sides was Sandu from the Midlands. The name suggested that it was a team comprising employees of S and U, a very successful company at the time, very much the brainchild of Clifford Coombes. Clifford was a cricketing fanatic, despite his advancing years, and his side was always sprinkled with some very good players and sometimes a professional footballer or two from the Midlands.

Clifford would invariably arrive some time after the start and as soon as he had changed into his whites, he donned the pads (and his other batting accoutrements) ready to stride to the wicket when the next man was out — regardless! The entrance to the ground is by way of a five-bar gate with concrete post on either side and somehow, in his keenness to bat early, Clifford managed to scrape the side of his Bentley. In all probability, Clifford had not driven into a field before with agricultural fencing.

I had been recruited to play against Sandu, taking a half-day of my annual holiday, and was keen to do battle but I was not exactly aware of the rules of engagement. This elderly gentleman (who had just caused major damage to his sparkling Bentley) took quite a while to get to the wicket and did not look completely at home after his uphill walk. The first ball was in the wicketkeeper's gloves before the batsman had moved, whereupon the wicketkeeper approached me at speed to ask if I had ever played against Sandu before. I said "No" whereupon he advised me of the ritual whereby the bowler was detailed to bowl an innocuous ball at

Clifford's bat, preferably down the leg side to allow a run to be taken as, if he scored, Clifford would pay for the teas! In such cases, it was always a pleasure to do so, not so much to get a free tea, but rather for the privilege of playing against such a splendid gentleman with a tremendous love of the game, who considered playing and getting enjoyment was so much more important than just winning.

In early September, we played quite a strong touring side, The Sou'Westers. I remember this game for two very good reasons. Our opening bowler was Duncan Short, who had faired extremely well when featuring in a North Devon touring side and quickly earned the nickname of "Drunken Duncan". The name was rather based on the effect of the odd pint rather than volume. He opened the bowling with great enthusiasm but he tended to have a rather open stance at the moment of delivery. As I was standing quite near to both the umpire and Duncan, the umpire awaited the next delivery which took Duncan out of earshot and promptly said to me "For God's sake, get the captain to take him off before he ruptures himself!" The scorebook suggests he lasted four overs.

I then got stick! A steady four pace run up caused few difficulties to those around me. This was followed by a positive shoulder movement, plenty of body action with the arm cutting away across the chest in the hope of some away movement on the odd occasion, or a tighter line with the arm coming down at the vertical with a twist of the body and a raising of the back foot to impart maximum spin. From nowhere came the call "No ball." I was not too sure how this came about, the umpire standing up tight to the wickets but I decided that my next delivery would be well inside the crease making absolutely sure that everything was right. I found this difficult as I began to realise that the umpire himself was not static and had a gentle nautical sway from left to right, a legacy from a celebration the night before and, being on tour, a beer or two at lunch time, particularly as he was not actually playing. Umpiring was much easier and less demanding on the body and mind than physically performing in the match, and could bear such luxuries. I got the call again "No ball" and the batsman, thinking it was his birthday, mustered all the strength he had to despatch the ball to the boundary.

I now had a two-fold problem, a swaying umpire dictating that I would have to time my delivery to coincide with his "away" sway, allowing me to deliver tight against the wickets, but this did not overcome the "No Ball" scenario. The time had come to confront him and to ask what I was doing wrong. "Lifting the back foot" was the reply. It was not a case of dragging it over the line or defaulting with the front foot, but at some stage as the arm cut across it became impossible to keep both feet on the ground — and so it is to this day. "Mr Sou' Wester", however, was not for turning and I remember finishing the over without a run up but delivering from a stationary position with absolutely no follow through! We drew, but I have never bowled so many "no-balls" in my life.

The season invariably ended with a formal dinner/dance which was always well attended. The New Inn provided a good venue and we were usually able to attract a good speaker from outside the district, which added to the occasion. The result was that the events were always well attended with representatives from other clubs, civic dignitaries, and friends generally — not always cricketers but supporters in the widest sense. Our illustrious scorer kept a scrapbook for each season and the ultimate pages would include the dinner toast list and a page (or two) set aside for the signatures of all those attending. In retrospect, these were splendid occasions enjoyed by one and all.

This particular year, I noticed the barely decipherable signature of one bearing the surname "Tucker". 'Awke and umpire Cecil Bird were great supporters of Plymouth Argyle and their trips to and from Plymouth became legendary for the stupidest of reasons. Something always happened. Folly Gate (a small hamlet to the north of Okehampton) became the half-way pit stop both to and from. Ale was supped and the two (sometimes joined by Ray Bird) would enjoy the company of mine host whom we all came to know as "Nod 'em in Tucker".

'Awke seemed to think that his battered old car would run for ever regardless and would never think of looking under the bonnet at any time. This was coupled with a reluctance to spend money and 'Awke had always been most careful in this department. 'Awke initially taught at "King Edward's, Totnes" (pronounced Tot-kneesssss) and later transferred to "St Jimmy's" (I never did find out the real name!) at Camelford, but both involved lengthy trips to and from Bideford each weekend so that he could partake in his beloved sports. In addition to cricket, 'Awke had been a rather impressive No.8 at rugby, and more latterly was the noisiest supporter of Plymouth Argyle AFC.

The car would run from Bideford to Totnes, there to be parked until the following weekend when the journey would be repeated. If 'Awke ran out of petrol (which he did more than once) he sent Cecil Bird (thirty years' his senior) off to get a quarter of a gallon — enough to see them home. On one occasion, they just made the garage, the attendant asked if 'Awke wanted his oil checked. This was the first time 'Awke had heard of this but thought the polite answer was "Yes".

The attendant took out the dipstick, showed it to 'Awke (who knew nothing about oil or that it was a necessary ingredient for the smooth running of any car) and said "There is no sign of any oil — shall I fill her up?"

"Can't you find me a longer dipstick?" was the immediate reply.

'Awke and Cecil went to watch one of the London sides play at Argyle and the linesman was non other than Roy Parsons, one of our former team-mates at Bideford who also ran the line in league soccer matches following his move out of the area to a more central location. Knowing that 'Awke and Cecil would be at

"Can't you find me a longer dipstick?"

the game, Roy looked them up and asked for a lift back to Bideford where he still had relatives and this would give him an opportunity of meeting up with them once again.

Came the pit stop at Folly Gate and the trio went into hostelry for refreshment. "Nod 'em in" said "The usual?" — of course — and then enquired who the visitor was. 'Awke explained that Roy had run the line at Argyle and this was an immediate invitation for "Nod 'em in" to recount one of his many tales. "Who were Argyle playing?"

"Leyton Orient" came the reply.

"My old team" said "Nod 'em in".

In time, 'Awke (and others) realised that form of conversation was the lead in to one of countless tales of super stardom from a wonderful storyteller which may have been true — or was it! The good storyteller always leaves an element of doubt.

"Played for them for a good many years — I was their star attraction. If ever I had a twinge or pulled muscle, nothing was said until two or three minutes from the start of the game otherwise the crowd would have upped and gone home. I was known as 'Nod 'em in'."

"How did you get a name like that?" asked our spellbound trio.

"Well, I used to play on the wing, and as I went racing along the touchline, I could hear the crowd saying 'It must be tied to his boot!' I would go around three or four, prod the ball towards the corner flag for one of my mates to collect, and then I would dash into the centre. Liked the ball on my head but if it did come in at boot level, I would flick it up into the air, one twist of the neck and the net was bulging — Nod 'em in Tucker had struck again!" 'Awke and Co. were mesmerised. There was nothing to suggest that this may not have happened — what a tale!

It was some time later that I played rugby at Plymouth — the last match of the season — and someone gave me a hospital pass, I was tackled from behind and fell to the ground right on the point of the shoulder. The

"Nod 'em in Tucker had struck again!"

grounds were like rock, there was a snap and in fact two of us shared an ambulance to the nearest hospital for bones to be set. My collarbone had gone. I had driven to the match in my car and when I rejoined the team, I arranged for someone else to drive home. I was unable to dress properly but had something resembling a cardigan which I put on over the sling. The lads were obviously looking for a night out and were somewhat concerned about me but I insisted that they have their fun and I would be happy to wait around. They decided to go back to Folly Gate. As soon as we walked in, I spotted "Nod 'em in" behind the bar.

He took one look at me and said "Not the old clavicle? I did mine at The White City in 1948." He went on to tell us all that he was in a top showjumping event at this world class venue and it came to the last round, and he needed a clear round to get the gold. Over the first fence, then the second, third and so on — the crowd was rapturous. On he went, cleared all the fences and then came to the last — he jumped it, the horse did not! Again, difficult to beat!

My abiding memory of "Nod 'em in" was when he turned up at our annual dinner, in DJ with hair parted right down the middle in Tommy Lawton style. He took the floor for a foxtrot, a very difficult dance, but he moved around the dance floor like a dream, toes turned slightly inward and he could well have been taking part in the finals of "Come Dancing". Maybe he had ridden at The White City, maybe he had earned the nickname "Nod 'em in" — whatever he was, he was a tremendous character and very good company.

1966 — Early on in the season, Somerset CCC were the visitors — a benefit match for Brian Langford. It is always a pleasure to be involved in this way, and on the day the weather was absolutely grand and Brian was well pleased with our support in his benefit year. Whilst there is an element of farce in that the spectators have come to see the county players "hammer" the locals, it is something to rub shoulders with those whose names appear daily in the summer newspapers as star players and in a way, everyone benefits.

It was also a chance to see a local boy, Brian Roe, whom I remembered as a young schoolboy playing against us, and here he was returning as a weathered professional to delight us all with his stroke play. There were others at that time who may have been equally gifted and one wonders what dizzy heights they may have reached had they enjoyed the same opportunities. As it was, we can only surmise though, I fear, many just would not have had the aptitude and stamina to play full-time cricket.

Playing in the game was Fred Rumsey, a left arm quickie who subsequently played for England. Max Lloyd, an opener for both Devon and Wiltshire and as such a senior Minor County batsman, told me how he had played against Fred in a serious game. Max opened the batting and told me that he had not seen one of the first six balls. This must be the frightening side of cricket — at the very top the bowlers are really fast allowing but a fraction of a second for the batsman to make up his mind as to whether to play the ball or not and having decided to get feet, body, head and hands in position to either defend or score. And to think that Denis Compton and the like would get in under such balls and hook them without helmets, visors and the other protective equipment they have today.

Brian Langford was presented with a cheque for just over £100, the spectators had had a wonderful time, and we had made many good friends. Brian asked me to look him up if ever I was at the County Ground and I did just that when the West Indian touring side were playing there. I smuggled in a bat and asked him to get the tourists and the home team to sign, which he did, though a number of the WI side seemed to write quite similarly but they may have had the same teacher!

The other good thing to come from the match was the fact that the clubhouse at Westward Ho! was repainted and the ground spruced up for this momentous occasion. It was also Sam Whalley's last match for us, the tax inspector had been promoted back to the Midlands. He had served us well as skipper and in one season scored eight hundred runs and took ninety wickets — a truly invaluable member of any team. Such quality players are not easy to replace.

The early part of the season was marked by low scores due, in no small measure, to frequent showers. Bowlers were in the ascendancy but this did not necessarily make for good or enjoyable cricket but usually called for drastic measures to reach a competitive total. Runs often came at the end of the innings when the long handle was applied. We also suffered from the absence of Mervyn Bird, our great left-hander, who did not appear until later on and immediately scored ninety-three runs, probably not even having had a net beforehand.

Our unfortunate opponents were Okehampton, a very good crowd of chaps to play against, but the game always followed a similar pattern. One felt rather sorry for our "quickies" as, after the fall of the first wicket, their best batsman, David Tucker, would come in, which was a sign that our skipper would immediately bring on the spinners. This was very disappointing if our opening bowler got an early wicket as he would immediately be taken off as David strode in. David was impressive and had played in representative games. His stout frame and strong arms had blasted many a good bowler out of sight but with the ball not coming onto the bat, against a slower bowler, a different technique was called for. If the bowler struck a good line and length early on, there was a very good chance that David would succumb. In our case, it seemed to work and it may be that David's eccentric habit of having to bang his right glove against his right leg immediately before each delivery, and the fact that he had very little time to do this against the slow bowler, with negligible run up, might have contributed to his downfall. This might have necessitated a hurried stroke which, against a turning ball, could be fatal. Anyhow, this was Bideford's theory, and it seemed to work.

The 30th July, 1966 was certainly a memorable day in more ways than one. Whilst cricket was all important and this was the cricket season, one had to have regard to the fact that the England soccer team was playing in the World Cup Final at Wembley against Germany, and this was not an occasion to be missed. The matter was quickly resolved. The cricket match at Westward Ho! was started earlier than usual — both teams retired to Mervyn Bird's pub in nearby Northam to watch the soccer — and it had been agreed that the cricket match should continue afterwards with a later finish. What initiative! The subsequent newspaper report suggested that the Wembley excitement had caused both teams to waver, Braunton rather more than Bideford, the latter running out winners by one wicket. It was rather nice that both codes could accommodate each other and certainly it was better than the cricket match being abandoned "soccer stopped play".

It is often said that "what goes around, comes around". A local newspaper headline at the time suggested that a miniature skyscraper of ten or more storeys was proposed for Westward Ho! in plans setting out the future proposals for the resort in an attempt to make Westward Ho! more attractive, with more trees, better roads and more car parks. During Council discussions, however, it was stated that the cricket ground should be preserved at all costs. This was comforting, though doubtless this would not be the last we should hear of such proposals to develop the ground, but the prophesy regarding the miniature skyscraper could well come true, a number of proposals being put forward during the early part of 2002.

It is sometimes extremely difficult to look back and recall some of the events which actually took place but there are certain landmarks which tend to stand out and are not easily forgotten. Newspaper reports remind me that Sunday 7th August and Monday 8th August, 1966, were rather special days in an aspiring off-spinner's lengthy journey. The Sunday was the return of Exeter Sunday Stragglers, a team we were pleased to receive from our county town, but, at the same time, whilst we may not have been destined for the Premier Division of the Devon Cricket League, we did fancy our chances and a visit by the Exeter premier side may have put us in our place and clearly shown that we had much to learn. *"The Stragglers had a fair sprinkling of goodish players, obviously strong enough to see the Westward Ho! upstarts off, but again it was not to be. Jared Collins, who had routed the visitors the previous year having taken six wickets for one run, followed this up with seven wickets for eleven runs, not one of the Exeter contingent getting into double figures".*

The next day, a welcome was extended to the Sheffield Cricket Lovers' Society, a very good cricketing side of up and coming players from the Sheffield area who seemed to speak a different language and certainly their attitude to cricket was so much different to our own. They absolutely lived for their cricket and exhibited a strength of purpose and application not expected in the south west. No one was in the side "to make up". The match proved quite extraordinary in that we won by ten wickets. SCLS won the toss and wasted no time in deciding to bat and were bowled out for eighty, the home side's two off-spinners doing the damage. There was no hurry when the home side batted, we had two technically sound batsmen who ground away and knocked off the runs without loss.

The SCLS went on to tour South Devon and, as usual for this team, at the end of the tour, they decided who were the best bowler and batsman encountered during that year. The bowling trophy came to Bideford for a *"five wickets for twenty-seven runs"* performance, *"which included three six hits in one over! This also was the bowler's one hundredth wicket mark for the season and fifteen hundred in total for the club".*

Newspaper reports can be misleading. Somehow our encounters with North Devon were interpreted dramatically in the local press, and perhaps they deserved to be so as they were always splendid, well contested encounters played in an atmosphere where every participant wanted to do well. The match played at Westward Ho! in August of this year was no exception, and the reports subsequently gave rise to letters to the editor questioning the reports.

North Devon won the toss, and the usual home ethic was to bat first, hopefully to get a large total thus putting immediate pressure on the team batting second, who would then have to score quickly on a wicket which had seen some wear.

Armed with four players having county experience, North Devon bucked the trend and invited Bideford to bat surely in the knowledge that if Bideford had not made sufficient runs by tea-time, they might bat on afterwards thus lessening the time North Devon would have at the crease to knock off the runs. And so it turned out to be. Bideford lost an early wicket and against quick and hostile bowling, battened down. The newspaper reports commented on the lack of aggression by the home batsmen but eventually (after tea) Bideford declared at one hundred and twenty-seven runs for the loss of eight wickets, after two and a half hours at the crease.

North Devon opened up with two of their county men and at sixty runs for the loss of two wickets, were going along nicely until panic set in and they lost six wickets for sixteen runs. The newspaper reported *"Then came the incident that will be discussed in the two clubs for years to come. With eight minutes to play, thirty-four runs were needed and the two batsmen added eleven runs in three minutes before one was caught on the boundary going for a six. With eleven runs to win and one wicket to fall, the umpire peered through the gloom at the pavilion clock to check the time. As the North Devon umpire ordered another over to start, Bideford skipper, Peter Williams, asked if the umpire had seen the clock, which by now had passed 7.30 p.m. The umpire had said that he had looked, and, probably because he was dazzled by the sun, thought there was time for another over. With the first ball of 'extra time', Mike Harrison was caught on the boundary to give Bideford victory"*.

Splendid stuff — a wonderful story, fit for the *"Hotspur"* or *"Rover"*, popular boys' comics circulating at the time.

Certainly the Bideford players were not aware of the "drama" as reported, but what a great end to a great match. Had the umpires relied upon their own watches, however, and not the pavilion clock, we might have had a drawn game. As it was, we did have a dramatic finale — you cannot get closer than producing a positive result in the final over.

The clock, incidentally, had been given to the club some years before by the then president and umpire, Captain Cope. It was at the end of the club's annual dinner. When a fair drop of ale and wine had been supped. Copey stood up to say that he thought it about time that the club had a clock on the outside of the changing rooms for all to see and for matches to be governed by. He went on to say that he would like to present the club with such a clock — he had one in his shed which unfortunately did not have any hands and was not working at that time, but he felt sure we could do something about it! Thank goodness for Pat Turner, the jeweller and clockmaker in our club — I am not sure if the original clock was repaired or whether we ended up with a "lookalike" but it was a definite improvement and a much needed facility.

1967 — The Annual General Meetings each year were auspicious occasions, though as we progressed there was need for changes to be made. We always seemed to have been blessed with good officers, well versed in procedures for such gatherings which were informative in the extreme. At one time, such meetings were held in The Town Hall — the Council Chamber no less — surrounded by large photographs of former Mayors of the Borough of Bideford looking down and influencing our debate and discussion. A notice was inserted in the local newspaper inviting all and sundry to come along, and, on occasions, they did! It was not uncommon, therefore, for the wife of one of the players to propose her friend's husband as captain (which was likely to be unopposed for fear of upsetting someone) and, following the election of the captain, the new captain's wife would return the compliment and propose the "captain proposer's husband" as vice-captain. Fortunately this was not a common practice throughout all the club XIs, but certainly some benefited (or otherwise) from this practice! Other posts were similarly manipulated and I well remember my first election as club secretary. I was fractionally late in arriving at the AGM (in the said Council Chamber) and as I walked in through the doorway, the chairman announced "And here is our new secretary." I made the point of being on time at future AGMs.

This year's AGM was certainly interesting — at least the newspaper report was — in that during the winter, the pitch had been invaded by moles and rabbits. Moles have not been regular visitors (they invariably were — and are — at Instow, the home of North Devon CC) but the situation can be combated necessitating the employment of "an expert". Local experts seem to have their own (and very peculiar) methods of catching such "varmints" who seem to know exactly where the playing area is and dig their tunnels towards the sacred turf, building up piles of earth along the way. This involves something akin to an underground railway along which the moles move with great alacrity, rather like a train (of the older variety), not staying too long in any one place. I think we were obliged to rely upon someone with big boots and puttees who was well versed in the ways of the mole and dealt competently with our problem. Fortunately, the moles have not returned in numbers since that prolonged winter campaign but we have to remain vigilant.

There was also an appeal for a scorers' hut. At one time, the scorers were accommodated in deck chairs strategically sited outside the changing rooms. It was certainly not an elevated position, there were constant passers by, but at least the wooden pavilion kept off the worst of the winds blowing in off the Atlantic. The appeal resulted in something akin to a garden shed being acquired with desk subsequently added. The scoreboard was the usual blackened board, riddled with nails to accommodate the metal plates with numbers painted thereon, and it leant against the outside of the score shed on match days. It was all very basic, as was much of our cricket. We acquired a new motor mower which, together with nets, had cost the club £52.

Early in the season, the club was bundled out of the North Devon Knock-Out Cup Competition by Littleham CC, a nondescript band of cricketers containing one or two "ringers". It was a total annihilation as far as Bideford was concerned with Brian Roe (of Barnstaple and Somerset fame) well to the fore with an immaculate innings backed up by a good and varied attack. Without our knowing, this was an introduction to some splendid and capable cricketers who would be joining us in a few years' time to form the basis of the club as we know it today.

We were joined by another P. Turner — one Pat the other Peter. Pat was a splendid character and no mean musician with his "Shadow" impressions. He was a more than useful all-rounder bowling a military medium pace gaining a little bit of swing in the Atlantic breezes; he was a renowned gully fielder (he truly made this a specialist position) and his batting was correct and thoughtful, though he languished at No.8 due to the strength around him. He was also the owner of an old Triumph car which seated quite a few in total comfort though his driving could be erratic mainly due to his feelings for all animals great and small, and swerving to miss the smallest of creatures was his forte. He nearly put us all through the windscreen for the sake of a rabbit on the way to Dulverton!

Pat sadly was the victim very much of his own misfortune when he took up hang-gliding. I recall that his initial experiences were in a field at Westleigh, where by running down the slope at the cricket ground, he would gain height and leave the ground for short flights which gave him great excitement and left him longing for more. I can quite imagine that progress was not fast enough for Pat but he soon graduated to the cliffs at Woolacombe along the North Devon coast. The truly sad thing was that one day, Pat did not tighten one of the nuts vital to his complicated piece of machinery and his launch off a high cliff was matched by an equally swift downward flight (if it could be called that) and Pat found himself hurtling towards a toilet many feet below. He didn't realise that he wanted to go that urgently! Pat crashed in a crumpled heap, many a bone smashed and his situation was certainly desperate.

Miraculously he recovered, I even persuaded him to speak to our local Rotary Club about his experiences, but thereafter he seemed unable to go far without his crutches, though his spirit never diminished and he could still see the funny side of things. I remember seeing him on the river front at Bideford one day as he passed my office on his crutches. As I went out to greet him, he started waving his crutches about frantically and said "I am waving these damned things about as fast as I can and I still can't bloody well take off!" An inner spirit such as that is very helpful indeed when you are up against it with cricket bat or ball, or yet life itself.

The other P. Turner, Peter, had attended Shebbear College and was a very competent cricketer, being a fluent quick bowler and hard hitting middle order batsman, scoring a century as early as May when the wickets are generally slow. A master at a nearby college, it gave the club a strong connection with the college which was so necessary as we were beginning to experience a shortage of players. The team generally had been together for a good many years and, like anyone else, cricketers do age without being prepared to acknowledge that they do.

I vaguely remember that, about this time, our esteemed PC "Noddy" suffered from vertigo having been struck by a cricket ball. This could well have been as a result of his fearless fielding at forward short leg a few feet from the bat, but newspaper reports say this was not so, but rather that he was hit on the cheek when batting against Barnstaple. The report goes on to say that despite his cheek immediately beginning to swell, Noddy stood his ground to face the next ball with the Bideford score standing at one hundred and ninety-nine runs for the loss of eight wickets. Noddy wanted to be there for the two hundred. Such was his disposition and rapidly altering facial expression that the Barnstaple bowlers refused to bowl to him. His own skipper asked him to leave the field to get medical attention and when he was reluctant to go, the skipper, Peter Williams, promptly announced his side's declaration! Noddy was then whisked off to hospital with a suspected fractured cheek. This confined Noddy to bed for a few weeks and we certainly missed his presence on the field and also his organisational ability. It was always said that, if there was a cancellation, Noddy could always raise a side from a call box outside his house, in about fifteen minutes flat. Many is the time that he has done just that.

I also remember going along to see how he was (I owed him this for his many years in menacing positions inches from the bat, often scaring the opposition into submission) and his wife invited me up to his bedroom to see him at first-hand. The room may have been a little small — it could have been that the bed was large — but I was obliged to stand on one side with little room on the other. I spoke to the prostrate Noddy, unable to lift his head from the pillow as this immediately awoke the dizziness and caused the room to spin. We had a steady and meaningful conversation about very little, but at least he was alive! His wife, a soundly constructed lady of considerable beauty and charm, came into the room and made across the bed to get to her bedside table. With every step, Noddy flew into the air, the ceiling whirled, he howled and he had just about enough time to land before the procedure started again. It was so funny had it not been serious, but I knew Noddy would be resolute and his general demeanour (when he landed!) told me that he would make a full recovery.

Towards the end of the season, we welcomed a

newcomer, Frank Twitchen, an ageing performer, worthy of comparison with James Bond when it came to prodigious feats. He was a firm believer that, as a bowler, it was his duty to get wickets, and if it was one wicket for thirty-five runs in three overs, he had done his bit. His enthusiasm and energy were rewarded when he received a trophy from a national newspaper for being the oldest competitive cricketer in the country — probably he was deserving of that. It is usual when a captain has a new player in his side to make enquiries as to the player's forte and what part he is going to play. Frank, when asked by 'Awke what he bowled, replied "Mixed bag!" Well now, how do you set a field for that? The situation was compounded when the first ball was despatched over the mid-off boundary for six!

Frank did not get downhearted, however, and was quick to recount that he had played cricket for a northern county against the very best and that in his early years, he was a most fearsome fast bowler. To add some credence to this (his "mixed bag" deliveries did little to suggest a former speed machine) he told the tale of how, many years ago, he had gone to a county match and had seen Harold Larwood going into the net for a bat. Harold was certainly the fastest bowler of his time and the most fearsome, at least, that is what we all thought. Frank asked Larwood if he would like him to throw down one or two to let him get his eye in. Larwood was delighted to have a willing bowler at his disposal and Frank, with limited run up, hastened to the wicket and let fly at the waiting Larwood. The ball whistled past his ear and Larwood was heard to pronounce "Good God, and I thought I was the world's fastest." Frank always told the tale with relish!

At over seventy years of age, Frank was still refereeing local school rugby matches and in after match celebrations would reminisce about playing centre three quarter inside the great Prince Obolensky, the England international rugby player, and giving him the ball at exactly the right time for an easy run in. Without Frank inside him, the Prince was only half the player! It was featured on TV that one international amateur boxer was about to have his seven hundredth bout; Frank remembered his seven hundred and first!

His war experiences were hair-raising to say the least, and it was fortunate for Churchill that Frank was able to mastermind the invasion of France. The storytelling was not malicious and there could always have been an element of truth but one thing was certain, here was a great character and the game was much richer for that. Of course, when Bill Shortridge bowled at one end and Frank the other, the batsmen were up against almost one hundred and forty years of experience, too much for any ordinary mortal!

Our usual fixture with North Devon at home was another classic — two very well matched sides battling it out with no little skill and certainly much determination. I remember the game for two good reasons — a lesser known middle order batsman saved the day for North Devon with a determined thirty-seven runs, only one of two North Devon batsmen to get into double figures, and a remarkable bowling performance by the home opening bowler due to considerable "prompting" by the visiting umpire!

Both sides always eye each other up, looking for the strengths and weaknesses and for the most part every wicket is important. There are always good bowlers who demand special attention and respect having regard to their speed or ability to flight and turn the ball. The odds (on this occasion) were slightly stacked in favour of North Devon who won the toss and decided to bat, probably to have first use of the wicket which could always deteriorate after tea, with little by way of patching being done to the wicket during the team interval when all participants were eagerly scoffing sandwiches and cakes in the nearby cafe. A quick brush of the wicket with a broom and possibly some more white lining to give the bowlers some idea where to let go of the ball and that was that.

Our opening bowler that day, Austin Dunn, had only recently joined us from another local club being what was politely termed "military medium" — not quick, but trundled along making use of wind and seam to generate a little movement. If the elements were not in support, as soon as the batsmen reached twenty runs without losing a wicket, Austin could well be consigned to the outfield — all such bowlers having reasonable "arms" to propel the ball somewhere near to where the wicketkeeper was standing, if this became necessary.

This was Austin's big moment, opening up the hill against North Devon CC. The ball was not new, but had been scrubbed and polished for the great event. It felt new and Austin clutched it in his rather large left hand whilst demonstrating to his new skipper exactly where he would like the fielders placed. This took rather longer than normal as, under pressure, Austin had a pronounced stutter, as the captain soon found out. "I'd like a m..mm..man there, and one.......there and so it went on until half the side was in position, the remainder awaiting a posting. Whilst doing this, the right hand would point while the left hand was still clutching, and when Austin had positioned about eight of his troops, a loud cry of "Dead Ball" went up. The match had not yet started but the astute visiting umpire had adjudged that after each posting, the right hand had joined the left (holding ball) and the umpire considered that he had spotted a little flourish before the right hand again pointed to the horizon. In his opinion, this constituted interference with the ball — a crime according to the laws of the game. Of course, this prompted a quick — well it should have been quick — response, the stutter became more pronounced, the language was extremely colourful — "What the f....f....f..." only the "f" came out! All this, and the game had not started!

Our immovable captain sought to bring reconciliation to the field of play and eventually it was agreed that the game should commence with Austin being assured that perhaps he had not really interfered with the ball at all. It may have been a ruse by the visitors to undermine confidence (this was always a fiercely contested fixture) but on the day it had exactly the opposite effect. Austin bowled like a dream, assisted by the onshore breezes, and he took five wickets for fifteen runs, a truly splendid performance. One often wonders how easily North Devon would have won the game without Austin being uplifted, but it was the visitors who were victorious by only five runs.

Another memorable encounter involving Austin took place at Ilfracombe. I could never understand it but Austin took great delight in his inability to bat and, having been out without scoring on quite a number of occasions, he started counting and amassed ten or so consecutive "ducks" prior to the Ilfracombe encounter. This fact was duly reported in the local press which did not really help the situation as Austin could well have been having thoughts about an entry in the *Guinness Book of Records*. Whilst his team-mates might have thought that additional runs were most important, Austin may well have had his eye in a totally different direction — another "duck" or two and instant fame!

At Ilfracombe, Austin was eventually called upon to bat when he came face to face with a great all-round sportsman who at one time had played for Bideford. He was an all-action player and great competitor who, on the afternoon, was anxious to add to his tally of wickets and became rather confident when confronted by Austin, having seen the press reports of Austin's recent poor form with the bat. The first two balls whistled past the bat and it was unclear as to whether or not they had been seen by Austin having regard to the way he reacted and the lack of direction on the part of his bat. The next ball was rather faster, it nicked the edge with Austin looking the other way, and it raced to the boundary for four.

"Lucky b....r" shouted the bowler. This was not received in the spirit in which it was given (or was it) when Austin started marching up the wicket towards the bowler waving his bat and shouting "Wh.... Wh.... What do 'e mean, lucky b....r? I'll wr... wr... wrap this bl...bl...bloody b-b-bat around your bl...y ear, when I catch you." What could have been a crime of passion was quickly averted and, with skills revived, Austin quickly forgot those ten previous fruitless encounters with the bat having found his true form once more.

The end of the season came all too quickly. The formal dinner/dance took place once again in November at an auspicious venue. There was something very nice about this in that we had a formal toast list and this particular year, the principal speaker was Nick Madgwick, from nearby North Devon CC, who had also played for Essex and Devon. Our chairman spoke as did 'Awke, who without a doubt was one of the most able and hilarious speakers one could possibly wish for. The Mayor of Bideford attended as did the Chairman of the Northam Urban District Council. Adjoining clubs were invited. It was an event not to be missed and in no small measure an appreciation by some of the local dignitaries that the club was something rather special, and not only on the cricket field.

1968 — Cracks started to appear both on and off the field. With hindsight, something should have been done to remedy the situation but with only one team and a following which virtually demanded good, attractive cricket at weekends this became increasingly difficult. Families became more affluent and mobile, and whereas Westward Ho! was the place to be on Sundays during the summer, standards had to be maintained otherwise alternative attractions might be found to be more desirable.

The club was losing money, only a relatively small amount by today's standards but it represented a downward trend. In addition, it was mentioned at the AGM that in recent years, we had lost fifteen to twenty staunch supporters. These were people who had followed the team through thick and thin, were always putting money into the green collection box which circulated around the ground at all home matches and had collected money from motorists as they had entered the gate.

At times during August, there had been difficulty in raising a team and, as such, fixtures for the coming season were to be reduced. How blind we must all have been. Here was something so well established, so vital at the time to Westward Ho! and we were rather more concerned with the past and immediate present rather than the future. At least we were becoming aware of the situation and hopefully would have the inner strength to do something about it. The secretary's comment at the AGM was that during the previous season, we had actually lost more matches than we had won. This included midweek matches where the strength of the side varied considerably but at the same time, the team was representative of the club.

Certainly the club was helped by guest players from other clubs when it came to midweek games against touring sides and this was probably good for North Devon cricket as a whole. A side from Swindon appeared with five Minor Counties players in their team and it was perhaps as well that two Barnstaple players guested for the home team and an excellent victory ensued.

Meanwhile, other North Devon sides were looking to take over the mantle of top side, none more so than Barnstaple Nondescripts who had an ex-Somerset opener, backed up by one of North Devon's best all-rounders, Rex Cudmore. I noted that at that time they also had Gerry Strothard, a superb wicketkeeper batsman, who had learnt his cricket well in the northern leagues and was certainly a "no nonsense" player.

As a keeper, Gerry set new standards and I recall that at Braunton he stood up to our quickie in a knockout match and whipped the bails off after gathering a ball at least a foot down the leg side. This would be a clear wide in today's game but it was something quite exceptional which one rarely sees outside the professional game and then certainly not off quick bowlers. His batting was merciless — the ball was there to be hit and when playing for North Devon, I have seen him hoist the ball out over the sea wall and onto the sands on many an occasion. Even that did not always bring a smile to his face!

My fondest memory of Gerry was when he played for Bideford at Plymouth Civil Service. We took a good side to Plymouth which included a young player subsequently destined to play professionally for Glamorgan though at the time (in my ignorance) I thought he was a better batsman! The Plymouth side had a very good pace bowler and, during the winter months, the wicket had been repaired and returfed where necessary, but this had been confined to the central areas of the wicket where the pace bowler pitched the ball. Young Tony and I did not use that part of the pitch at all, we dropped the ball much nearer the wicket which had not been treated or extensively repaired as had the centre portion. The result was chaos. The well pitched up ball turned at right angles and it was goodbye Plymouth! Our captain had spotted this and very quickly brought the spinners on. The situation was not helped by Gerry standing right up, bristling with anticipation, and ready to do a good day's work. He was not averse to advising the batsmen right at the beginning that the wicket was unplayable and that it was not going to be their day!

In no time the ball was turning sharply and the young opening bat was having a torrid time against the turning ball. In the end, he succumbed to a ball which must have turned a foot or so from outside the off stump and took middle. The disgruntled batsman turned to Gerry and said "It isn't fair, he isn't bowling straight."

"Straight enough to hit your bloody wicket — on your bike!" Gerry must have come from Yorkshire!

Ray Bird scored his second "ton" for the club, the first having been ten years before. This probably does not convey much, Ray being an opening bat, and perhaps it may even have been a bit disappointing in that he went ten years without achieving that figure though, doubtless, he had tried week by week. Ray's real strength was that he was a clubman supreme in that the club always came first. Whilst the object of opening was to see off the opponents' prime strike bowlers, if Ray happened to open with someone who chose to defend rather than also look for runs, it was Ray who chanced his arm though this was not his natural game. If we knew we needed runs quickly and time was short, it was Ray who dropped himself down the order for the sake of the team.

He looked after his bowlers, and, as a captain, no match ever got out of hand. Many is the time that our opponents got off to a good start but somehow you could feel the stranglehold on and once the breakthrough came, the field would gradually close in without it being too obvious, and the wickets would begin to fall regularly. He would always look after his bowlers and do what was best for the team and them.

Such a man was probably summed up on the day we played against North Devon at Westward Ho! Our ageing spinner, Bill Shortridge, was not in fact selected but turned up to a full and expectant changing room where the members of the home team were getting ready for the fray. This was at a time when players were notified of selection by postcard. Bill burst into the rather small room and announced that whilst he had not actually received a card, he always played against North Devon and touring sides and obviously his card had been lost in the post! Ray immediately decided to step down to avoid causing anyone any embarrassment, whereupon most of the players expressed the same sentiment as Ray was indispensable when it came to tactics and knowledge of the game generally. I cannot remember the outcome of the game, but Ray played, I know we would have given a good account of ourselves and someone missed out, but it was obvious that Ray's heart was equally as big as his frame and the team would follow him anywhere.

It seems strange how the North Devon CC games come to the fore but such was the intensity of such encounters and the characters involved, that few games lacked something most unexpected. The mid-August fixture at Instow was no exception. North Devon had three county players, all of whom fared well in the batting stakes, including Bill Shepherd, the very fine left-handed all-rounder, who passed his one thousand runs for the season in a "not out" performance.

The home side, however, took rather a long time to get the one hundred and thirty-six runs for the loss of eight wickets leaving the visitors with less than two hours' batting on a wicket which had given the bowlers some encouragement. Bideford's early batsmen were no match for the spin/speed combination of the two county men, and within less than an hour, the score stood at thirty-eight runs with five wickets down. It was then that one could see the value of good (and perhaps merciless) captaincy.

The home skipper changed the bowling, put himself on and, in the next six overs, fifty-six additional runs were scored off the bat. A stand of eighty-six in forty-nine minutes by Mike Sparrey and Jared Collins did the damage, Bideford knocking off the runs for the loss of six wickets. Mike hit four sixes in his fifty-six not out (he had previously taken three cheap wickets), one of them, I remember, was a full toss which he hit straight out of the ground. A six at Instow is a big hit, four in an innings would severely damage the reputation of any bowler. Mike was that sort of explosive cricketer, he was always in the game, and a quite exceptional fielder with a wonderful pair of hands. He was eventually rewarded in later years when he was selected to play for the county over 50s where he continued to perform effectively.

In mid-August, we played against a spirited Barnstaple side which just happened to have someone in the team who played the drums in a local band. He had a gig that evening but had agreed to make up the side provided he could get away early. Bideford batted first and the only way the drummer could get away early was to open the batting. Bideford, in turn, quickly brought on Bill Shortridge ("Two spin Hagen" as 'Awke referred to him) with his high-flighted leggers and with a sprinkling of "offers" thrown in. It was a nightmare for any fielder within about twenty yards, as Bill was a firm believer that if someone whacked you, the next ball should go even higher and slower. It was quite disturbing if you happened to be fielding close in (it did happen now and again) as you daren't look at the bowler, but had to be content with staring at the bat just wondering what was going to happen next. It was alarming when you saw the batsman's eyes light up, his feet would start to dance and the bat would be raised very swiftly indeed.

And so it was this evening. "Mr Drummer" did just that — eyes lit up, feet danced and he let fly — in fact he had great difficulty in missing the ball and played his best innings of the season. In the end, I believe he was obliged to surrender due to his band commitment but Bill clearly thought that he had outwitted "Mr Drummer", leaving him a nervous wreck and totally drained after facing such a beguiling performance.

The season ended on quite a high note with Mike Sparrey continuing to shine as an all-rounder with some excellent performances. Against Exwick, his strong arms accounted for six sixes in an innings of fifty-four before taking four cheap wickets. One of these was a fine young batsman who subsequently played against Bideford some thirty-four years later, still batting with great style and panache.

The season ended with the annual dinner, once again in august surroundings, and it was pleasing to note that Mrs Ethelwynne J. Brown once again attended, the former mayor whom 'Awke had addressed as "Mrs Thing-a-me-bob". She must have enjoyed her first visit so much that she was not going to miss a second! Jared Collins had topped the batting and bowling averages but claimed that it was not without much physical pain and suffering!

Coaching in this part of the county was nigh non-existent unless one went to a particularly fashionable school. At the local grammar school, the master in charge of cricket organised the house matches (we played two in one day!) and there were a few fixtures.

Wednesday was sports afternoon and two individuals were chosen as captains and went along the ranks of the remainder, choosing a select XI each. Those not chosen would sit on the grass and watch. There was no question of wearing whites although we were permitted to wear plimsolls which made for dainty footwork. That was it. We amused ourselves (if you were fortunate enough to be chosen) with batters trying to hit the ball as hard as possible, and bowlers trying to bowl as fast as possible — all conducive to good and attractive cricket!

Some boys were naturally talented in all sports and could be relied upon to produce something, but others were mere fodder, not understanding even the basics. I was somewhere in between.

During the winter months prior to the coming season, a new incentive was launched. There was going to be some organised coaching in North Devon to be undertaken by one of North Devon CC's leading lights with vast knowledge of the game, having played for both Essex and Devon. As a headteacher, he was to be respected and despite now advancing years, I decided to enrol. Imagine, as a relatively seasoned player and somewhat battle scarred, lesson number one was as basic as learning how to pick up and hold a cricket bat. In all honesty, this was something completely new to me — the bat was some kind of weapon to be wielded menacingly hoping to make contact with the red ball now and again to advantage. I suddenly became aware that there was something more to it than that. By picking up the bat from the floor in the right way and slightly adjusting my hands, I felt a degree of comfort and with appropriate criticism, realised that not every ball was actually on or just outside my off stump (as it had always seemed to be) but there were balls on the leg side which could be despatched if the correct movements were followed. The bat also played a part in defending one's wicket, something that I had not previously thought of!

Batting became more of a challenge though I realised it was far too late to make a real impression as a batsman, though principally being a bowler, I found much more joy and satisfaction in scoring runs rather than getting wickets. I am not sure why, but batting in its way could become quite artistic.

The winter sessions went well until one unpleasant evening, two of the lads from a particularly rural club, raised certain questions which had been bothering them. We had reached the stage when our coach decided to show us how to play the back foot defensive shot. This was demonstrated without ball and with all the appropriate grace, but Rural Player No.1 asked how did you play such a shot in front of your face (a quite normal requirement on his home pitch). It obviously was not possible to get one's elbow that high. Rural Player No.1 was disappointed that our illustrious coach could not provide an answer to every problem and, as this was the type of ball he would face week after week, it was pointless carrying on if he could not be equipped for all eventualities.

We then had a session when bowling was to the fore, and the coach ran through the grips to produce the various types of delivery. I have always found that quality bowlers have something that little bit extra built in, but everyone has to start somewhere. Rural Player No.2 asked what was the grip for the shooter! As politely as possible, the coach advised that there was no such ball, though spinners sometimes bowled the top spinner which hastened through and kept a little lower. Rural Player No.2 was not impressed and said that his team had a player who bowled a shooter week in, week out. Things got a little bit ruffled and our numbers dropped once again!

I only played on this particularly rural pitch on the one occasion. It sloped appreciably and I do remember that our quickest bowler marked out the end of his run amidst some cabbages adjoining the boundary. The back foot defensive shot in front of the face was very much in evidence but I cannot remember seeing "the shooter" on that memorable day.

1969 — Younger players were coming through and were awarded trophies for their progress during the previous season. We also saw the passing of two great stalwart supporters both of whom made bequests to the club of £50. This was not an inconsiderable sum in those days and the gifts were gratefully received. One was "Copey", an outstanding umpire and colourful character who presided over the club's activities for a good many years. He was colourful in more ways than one with his sun blind blazer and shooting stick and, for the final game in each season, he would dress appropriately in black signifying the death of another season.

Dave King joined the club from Barnstaple and added considerable strength to the batting line up. A great "watcher" of the ball and always batting well within his crease he expected to hit every ball absolutely in the middle of the bat and if he did not do so, even if the ball went for four, he showed his disappointment when beginning to run between the wickets. He was an absolute perfectionist and would have done well in whatever company. In twenty-two innings he scored almost one thousand runs, at an average of just below sixty.

The home wicket, where most matches were played, was not a particularly good one with some hope for any type of bowler, but such was the quality of his batting and style, there would always be the bad ball and this would receive its just deserts. I well remember a Sussex County first teamer playing at Westward Ho! guesting for a side from South Devon. As an opening bowler (not the fastest but cutting the ball away regularly), he bowled slightly short, probably hoping for more lift, and Dave simply took him apart. It did not matter who the bowler was, the good balls were stopped, the bad balls stroked away and a slightly short ball to someone taking his guard well back inside the crease, presented the bowler with a problem rather than the batsman.

One of the most momentous occasions during the season was the granting of a twenty-eight year lease by the Council to the cricket club. This was a must as far as grants and long term planning were concerned.

The facilities at the ground, up until this time, had been primitive in the extreme, and wooden floors and wooden bench seats in the changing rooms were not helpful in a somewhat restricted atmosphere. Splinters were a common hazard both here and in other wooden establishments. For many years, a "bum splinter" was on display in the changing room alongside the bat rack. It was a vicious looking sliver extracted, not without considerable skill, by Roy Bird who thereafter was regarded as JEC's best friend! Doubtless many suffered a similar affliction and often in silence.

The new lease may not have been that significant to many but it meant the possible end of the wooden hut where all twenty-two players could certainly not change all at once. There might be the prospect of running water and even showers being incorporated in any new structure. Visits to the nearby cafe for tea might also become a thing of the past and, who knows, there might even be a bar where the game might often be replayed in the evening twilight. Such a dream seemed all too far away.

At this stage in the proceedings, we were joined by Terry Josling. A colourful character by any stretch of the imagination, his cricket and his approach to the game did not come from any manual though he was always able to leave an impression. Never lacking in confidence, he seemed to regard most batsmen as idiots (perhaps a good approach for any aspiring bowler) and, whilst initially bowling medium pacers which did a little bit either way, he eventually settled back into the lofted delivery which encouraged a dancing of feet. Such was the time it took the ball to arrive, I firmly believe the batsmen had time to look at Terry before playing the ball, could see the look of triumph in his eye, and made a mess of the subsequent strike. Even the best seemed to fall for the evil plan and Terry took some very good wickets.

He also had a good pair of hands (particularly to his own bowling) and his batting was the result of having the same attitude to the bowler as he had for the batsmen — not very good. Colourful tales suggested that all the local bookmakers were on a losing wicket with Terry and his triumphs in the betting stakes became legendary, without any firm evidence! Colourful was the only word for him.

He was also no mean soccer player and from a very young age was what one might term "solidly built". This gave him a sound base and in the penalty area, he was all backside and elbows as he went for the ball.

If you wanted to liven up any changing room, one could always mention the time Bideford Colts (Under 18) XI won the County Knockout Cup at St James' Park, Exeter (Exeter City's very own ground) in 1951. Terry was lethal with his head and fortunately the team had two very good wingers, one of whom played for Liverpool the following season. The opposing centre back marking Terry subsequently played as a professional in the Football League, but on the day, Terry performed extremely well, being in the right spot at the right time, arriving in the penalty area just as the crosses came in. The would-be pro was nowhere to be seen. Bideford won the game 5—2 and the newspaper report mentioned one or two of the Bideford players who had dashed about and also the up and coming professional marking Terry.

It had been a good and entertaining game with plenty of action and the write-up ended with the comment (almost as an afterthought) that *"Josling scored five!"* Otherwise, it was just as if Terry was not there, but scoring all five goals was a prodigious feat which we all appreciated even if the press had not. Terry is always very happy to be reminded of this being one of the highlights of his sporting life and he is similarly happy to give his own "colourful" description of what actually happened on the day!

Wins were not quite so easy to come by as in the past, notwithstanding the excellence of our two best batsmen. Meanwhile, the bowlers performed manfully with the wickets being shared.

In looking back, one must wonder how some of the cricketers of the 1960s would fare in the competitive atmosphere of League cricket in the early 2000s. The major difference surely must be the depth of the batting, improved techniques brought about by coaching, and the gradual raising of team scores in local cricket to an average of two hundred runs per innings. Much of this could be attributed to greater attention being given to the preparation of the wickets which, in some leagues, are regularly inspected and assessed. The fact that new cricket balls are produced for each game (and in some cases each innings) must also be a factor.

On the bowling side, there have always been good bowlers and these would adapt more easily, the result being that a good bowler will still produce a good average over a season. Bowling up and down is no longer an option, the bowler must do something with the ball either in the air or off the pitch to secure wickets and there have always been those capable of doing this. Very few batsmen now give their wickets away, all wickets have to be earned.

The weekend players at Westward Ho! were rather more than just cricketers. Many were very firm friends and we spent much of our leisure time together. We all had business or teaching careers to pursue and cricket was very much a way of getting away from the daily pressures into a land of fantasy and nonsense where we could get rid of excess energy and have considerable enjoyment at the same time.

One such remarkable gentleman was Roy Bird. At one time an agricultural salesman, a few sudden deaths up the line and his natural ability soon groomed him for managerial success. In such a capacity he was not always available to many of his workers yet Roy liked to identify himself with those at the pit face, so to speak. He had moved to take over a new local branch of agricultural merchants and was working late one evening when the telephone rang. Being the last to leave the premises, Roy was on his own and so took the call. It was one of his lorry drivers who had found himself in a ditch about three miles from base. He asked that someone should come and fetch him. Roy quickly acquainted the driver with the fact that he was speaking to the manager, that there was no one else available, and that the driver would have to fend for himself. The driver pleaded that it was only three miles, he had a wife and children waiting for him at home, and they would be worrying if he did not return very shortly. Roy, a man with a heart of gold, asked where the lorry was and set off to rescue his driver.

In no time, the driver was found and on board. It was a wonderful November evening, dark and crisp, cloudless and with full moon. This was the opportunity of a lifetime for the driver, alone in a car with his boss — what a time to impress. He immediately struck up a conversation, in his strong Devonshire accent, and thought the subject should be topical.

Perhaps I should mention here that it was at the time when the Russians had sent a rocket into space, causing consternation worldwide as so little seemed to be known about the galaxy and outer space.

"Lovely moon up there, Mr Bird."

"Yes" answered Roy.

"Bit worried about these yer Russians sending these yer rockets up to the moon."

"Yes."

"Supposin' there's someone living up there?"

"Well, there could be."

"Supposin' they don't like it and start a war."

"I hadn't thought about that."

"I 'naw whose side I'd rather be on — they'm fighting downhill!"

It is difficult not to laugh in such circumstances and Roy did restrain himself, but every time there is a full moon, I look upwards and can quite understand the logic behind the driver's argument!

My venture along the club highway up until this point has been greatly assisted by the comprehensive scrapbooks meticulously assembled by our lady scorer and to this extent, this is perhaps the end of an era. Scorebooks were basically the same as they are today (less one or two refinements) but I recall that the compilation of averages for the season was something else. All club matches were featured, there was no such thing as League cricket, so that in a sense all matches were "friendlies" and played in an appropriate spirit. The preparation of the averages consisted of systematically going through all the matches for the season with headings for each batsman and bowler and adding a score or bowling figures for every performance. At the end of the day, the figures had to be totalled and, whilst some offices did have adding machines, these were primitive and the very best had a handle at the side which had to be depressed as each entry was made. It was a mammoth task quite unlike the shifting around of figures on a computer screen and one which brought little reward except for those who had the gratification of topping the averages. Sadly, we seem to have gone away from this and with league tables and team sheets, averages for individual competitions are maintained elsewhere and are not always available to a club. In a way, more's the pity as so much of our past history has been lost but then, averages aren't everything.

My greatest fan and supporter was my grandad. Whilst his wife was alive, the two of them would come to Westward Ho! and lean against the top fence every Sunday to watch one of their grandsons (he may have been the favourite!) play for the home team. Grandma carried excessive weight and had great difficulty in walking very far, if at all, but she was able to get out of the car, cross the road, and station herself in a prime position along the top fence where the wooden rails were affixed at a convenient height for leaning and the boundary was not too far from the wicket. Grandad, on the other hand, was razor slim, with a heart of gold, and he too enjoyed the Sunday trips. I did not realise exactly how much. Both were wonderful people with whom I lived during part of my earliest days and so there was a special bond. I did not really appreciate the extent of this until much later in life.

When Grandad became a widower, he lived on his own in the family house, and as vice president of the cricket club, he would get a fixture card each year setting out the games which had been arranged both home and away. I would have to say little else to him but every Saturday and Sunday during the season, I would go along to his town house and he would be standing there in his porch with sandwiches neatly packed into a box awaiting my arrival. He was a meticulous man and always brought a notebook in which appropriate notes were made as the games progressed. I would drive him into a good position at the ground so that he could see all the action from the car, unless he preferred a seat when the weather did the unexpected and the sun shone.

The team all knew when Grandad was there and would go along and have a word with him, commenting on the match and often gently ribbing him about his favourite grandson. One, Peter Williams, was particularly adept at this and I remember the time when a local slogger (a regular visitor to Westward Ho! and well known to us all) hit out unashamedly and actually made contact. I did the silly thing and bowled wicket to wicket to try and bowl him out which, in such a belligerent mood, was absolutely stupid. Had I bowled wide, his stroke would have been exactly the same with a very good chance that the ball would have spooned up into the air for a catch. On this particular day, the ball cleared the boundary on more than one occasion and Peter was quick to sidle up to Grandad and say "JEC certainly got stick today."

"All luck" replied Grandad, "I could see the batsman had his eyes closed from here." Good old Grandad, I wish I could have lived up to his expectations.

It was not until his death in early 1970 that I was handed a blue covered scrapbook full of newspaper cuttings covering the period 1949-1969. They were not all of myself nor yet of the cricket club, but there were other cuttings of achievements by other members of the family. The bulk of the book, however, was about cricket and it was then that I realised that after every match, Grandad would look through the local newspapers for reports for his scrapbook and, in many instances, he recorded my efforts ball by ball, and then would compile his record of events.

Deep down, I wish I had really thought how much it meant to my Grandad picking him up and taking him to cricket every Saturday and Sunday during the season, but then again, what else could I have done had I known.

The scrapbooks (and those of our official scorer) prompted me to put pen to paper in an attempt to record the happiness which our cricketing activities at Westward Ho! brought to so many between 1949 and 1969, including the players, spectators and our visitors.

Perhaps, therefore, this is the time to finish. It was the end of an era for a good many reasons but not the end of cricket at Westward Ho! A great period of change was in the offing — a new clubhouse, League cricket, more encouragement for younger players and the formation of colts sections by all the leading clubs. All these matters were for the good of the game, but something seemed to have been lost. Leagues and points introduced an edge. Overseas players have become the norm, there have been changes in the laws, and many restrictions introduced as regards overs to be bowled, whilst the batters can carry on scoring to their hearts' content. I digress.

In following Grandad's record of events, I have not mentioned three other areas from which I have derived great enjoyment over the years. The first are incidents not actually involving my own club; the second — a small intrusion into Minor Counties cricket which, surprisingly, seemed to attract the same amount of nonsense as club cricket but on a slightly different plain, and thirdly, The cricketing tourist.

Cricketing Extras — Other Clubs — Life at times does not seem to be fair and I have come across players with great natural talent who do not seem very interested in cultivating that talent to a higher level. At the other end of the scale are those totally immersed in the game of cricket who are not very good players and who are happy to bat at No.11, do not get a bowl, but enjoy the chase for the ball around the field during an innings. I cannot think of any other game where so many people fall into this category.

On occasions, I have been invited to attend the post season dinners organised by various clubs in the area. Standards varied but all were enjoyable and it was always good to be amongst friends. Alwington CC always insisted that all their members should wear club ties at the Annual Dinner under pain of a fine for not doing so. One member, however, never wore a tie although he was one of the staunchest members though rarely bowling and always batting at No.10 or 11. He was quite happy to pay the fine until such time as he scored ten runs in an innings and then he would feel justified in wearing and honouring the club tie. I was more than delighted to be bowling when he scored that tenth run and looked forward to the next Annual Dinner when he would be properly dressed and not be fined. Someone remarked on that evening that if a law was passed making the game illegal, Jack Wickett would hang himself! What is more, he meant it. Does any other game attract such passion?

The same club had several very good players who would have graced far better teams but the club was well founded and most members of the team seemed to be related to one another by birth or marriage. This did much to keep the team together. With the better players "on song", the team could cause an upset or two, and Billy Walter went on to star for the North Devon CC both as a bowler and a batsman. He did play for

140

the county but, sadly, his limited county performances did not do justice to a supreme natural talent. With a couple of other good batsmen, the team could rattle up a good score to give Bill something to play with and with his extra pace and bounce, runs were never easy to come by.

In one of its better years, Alwington CC reached the advanced stages of the local knockout cup which resulted in a visit to the sacred ground at Instow to play against the home side, North Devon CC. This was at a time when the home attack was spearheaded by Mike Jaquiss, still the fastest bowler in North Devon.

Alwington were putting on a particularly brave show and the quality batsmen enjoyed playing on such a good, fast wicket and basically did quite well though it was a limited overs match and risks had to be taken. They were, and whilst the score steadily grew so did the fall of the wickets. I found myself in the visitors' changing room urging on the troops against a higher calibre side and when the star batsmen had duly performed, the tail-enders were expected to come in and hit a boundary or two to give the opposition something exciting to chase.

Batting fairly low down for Alwington was Johno Osborne. Keenness was his main asset but perhaps he was a little out of his depth in such prime company and on such a fine, true wicket. He knew that Mike still had overs in hand and that ultimately they would meet but meanwhile he was bracing himself ready for the fray. "I am not afraid of Mike Jaquiss — he won't bother me." "Fast — I have faced fast men before." "What have I got a bat for?" This psyching up was most impressive and showed stomach for the fight.

When eventually the next wicket fell, Johno strode manfully from the thatched pavilion, through the congregating members, and he was half-way to the wicket when someone shouted "What about your pads?" Johno stopped, actually looked down as he was still in a self-induced trance, and low and behold, he had forgotten to put his pads on so anxious was he to face

141

North Devon's fastest bowler! He had to rush back into the pavilion, the build up was lost in the fray, and it was a bit of a wreck who eventually reached the wicket to be sacrificed to the quick bowler. I think we all felt for Johno, but the memory remains etched in the minds of all those sympathetic supporters present that evening.

Whilst I have club Annual Dinners in mind, later on, after the Bideford & Westward Ho! CC merged with Littleham CC to form the Bideford, Littleham & Westward Ho! CC, a major transformation was brought about as not only was there an influx of new and younger players, but some excellent administrators and communicators. Good links were maintained with most clubs and hopefully these continue to the present day, but with the joining of the two clubs, there was a much wider range of clubs involved and new friends to be made.

Almost one of my first introductions to clubs formerly on the Littleham list, was when I accompanied our new chairman to the Annual Dinner of a club near Tiverton. Following a sumptuous meal, various presentations were made, including one to an opening bat who received an award for taking part in the biggest stand of the season. The young player rose and made his way to the top table to receive his trophy and whilst he was shaking hands, the presenter went on to explain to the assembled mass that "the biggest stand" referred to was behind the pavilion after the match against.........!

Whilst not wishing to intrude on the hereafter (the amalgamation), there were some very special trips to be undertaken and the top of the "special" list was certainly the game at Bridgetown. The local club was a reasonably good country team but the ground was something very special being on the fringes of Exmoor. It might almost have been regarded as a 2nd XI fixture but the hosts were not a bad side at all and so the fixture became associated with Reg Rawle, a magnificent gentleman, clubman and captain, who always strove to bring any match he played in to a conclusion in the last over, with a positive result. He never took the field without his cap — tucked away in his back pocket!

It became the thing to be chosen to play for "Reg Rawle and his Picnickers". This privilege fell to me on one very memorable occasion. We processed in convoy across Exmoor and stopped alongside a tranquil river a few miles from Bridgetown where we had a picnic lunch (hence the name of the tourists). At the right time of the year, this eliminates all thoughts of cricket and bat on ball and it is quite easy to doze off with the sun at its height. Reg would then rally his troops for the final leg of the journey, following the said river to its higher reaches along a tree strewn valley. The scenery is magnificent and beyond the trees, and with a hilly backdrop, is the Bridgetown cricket pitch. Parking is further along from the ground beside a nearby pub and then we were obliged to walk a relatively short distance to the single file pedestrian bridge leading over the river and onto the ground. Cricket bags had to be carried in elongated fashion in front of the body over this quaint wooden structure. The ground itself is a lesson in topography with level grassed areas, the bounding river and, on the far side, something resembling the foothills of Nepal at the approaches to Everest. Half-way up the hill stood a small but beautifully thatched hut which doubled as a changing room and score hut. It was one of those establishments where one had to draw lots as to who should change first. I was impressed.

When it became my turn to change, I entered the august building to see a copy of an old-fashioned telegram pinned to the wall. Remembering that this was in the 1970s, the telegram was addressed to Colin Cowdrey, wishing him well in his first test match for England against the West Indies to be played at Bridgetown, BARBADOS! It gave the changing room atmosphere.

Playing on a ground like this was not without its hazards for players and spectators alike. We batted first and on occasion, the ball ended up in the river, but a net and enthusiastic dog were both in attendance and earned their keep as the afternoon progressed. The deteriorating quality of the ball did not seem to deter the home attack but I did not relish trying to spin a ball which was becoming progressively wet, unless, of course, there was another ball set aside for the second innings.

The runs steadily mounted interspersed with an unexpected wicket or two when the ball rapped the pads. A couple of our best batsmen received this treatment and at the end of the innings, four were not over pleased with their "lb ferkins" ('Awke's expression for LBW!). Teatime came with one hundred and forty-seven on the board — perhaps enough, if we were able to strike early and take a wicket.

Towards the end of the innings, Reg played defiantly and almost hit a four. The then president of the club (a retired professional journalist with a wonderful turn of phrase) was very often highly critical of Reg and suggested that he might do better if he played more positively and did away with the "honeymoon shot". Reg was not a great striker of the ball — he always advocated a high backlift, but the downward strike was much slower and at times did not coincide with the arrival of the ball. When there was contact, the bat speed was in single figures with a decided lack in propulsion so that boundaries were a rarity without a slope to assist. The president's rapid analysis of Reg's batting art form meant little without a definition of "honeymoon shot", and when asked to enlighten us as to what this was, *El Presidente* would reply "The tentative prod!" We all understood.

At Bridgetown that day, Reg played one remarkable shot, full of power and precision and, whilst it was destined for the cover boundary, the ball had to make headway up the foothills. Cover point stood where he was, the ball shot past him towards the boundary and then gently arched around back to where the cover was standing whilst Reg scrambled a two.

During the team interval, one of our ladies asked

where the nearest toilet was. It was at the pub, across the bridge and some way back along the road. The local inhabitant apologised profusely and asked if our lady could come again next year by which time, the home club hoped they would have a "Jubiloo", to commemorate the Queen's accession to the throne!

A sumptuous cream tea followed and it was then time for us to take the field. It was not unusual for me to have a word with my great friend, Andy the keeper, to sum up the elements, the lie of the pitch and other factors in case the captain asked if I had a preference as to which end I would like to bowl.

Walking out together, Andy and I turned around to see the umpires coming out and I raised the point that the home umpire had taken on a different appearance from the one who had said "Yes" to four LBW appeals in the first innings. The keeper was not too sure and so I decided to make conversation with the gent who might possibly be standing at my end, if and when the captain decided that I might bowl.

"Good afternoon, Mr Umpire — were you standing for the first innings?"

"Nope" came the reply after the umpire removed the strand of grass from between his teeth.

"Is the other umpire all right — has he been taken ill, or something?"

"Nope."

"Why isn't he umpiring the second innings?"

"Cos he's just got his 100th LBW of the season."

I could not let the occasion pass and said "How splendid, if a bowler gets one hundred wickets a season or a batsman one thousand runs in a season, they usually get an award at the Annual Dinner — surely the umpire should get something for a hundred LBWs."

"He does" came the reply, "and this will be his fourth consecutive season!"

What a precedence this could set if word got around!

We just about managed to win a very exciting match but I shall not forget one over when I managed to get two wickets, broke a finger, and was hit for two sixes into the river. Bowling with a wet ball was not easy.

It was a few years later that, professionally, I was asked to dispose of a property on behalf of a London solicitor and she happened to live at Bridgetown. I went along to see her and her property actually overlooked the cricket ground which adjoined her property. Her husband had been a keen cricketer and so the property had a great many attractions in addition to the exquisite scenery. A suggestion when she purchased the property was that she would be responsible for the preparation of teas for the home cricket matches. I know she took this obligation seriously enough though she could well have delegated some of her responsibilities to the many willing helpers, particularly as her profession often required her presence in the capital city.

Another game which did not fall within the club arena was one particular representative match which was played at Plymouth in 1968. It took the form of a county trial to allow the county selectors an opportunity of seeing what was on offer in various parts of the county. As was to be expected, the team from the north of the county contained a number of players from North Devon CC, some of whom were already county players, and a few odds and ends from the smaller clubs, but nevertheless capable of holding their own. No representative side from the north could be without Mike Jaquiss, our quickest bowler, and the side was captained by the county opening batsman from Mike's club.

We were changing apprehensively when in burst Andy Scott, a tall, athletic young man few of us had heard of, and he brazenly introduced himself by saying "And who was the fastest bowler before I arrived?" This was not something to be said in front of Mike J, who was really quick.

We fielded first and Andy immediately lost confidence in his skipper for the day when he was not chosen to open the bowling, or perhaps it was just that his captain was deaf! Mike marked out his run which drew a gasp from Andy who was stationed in a fielding position close to the bat. I suspect that Mike added a pace or two which was not good news for the batsmen. Having had his bluff called, when Andy was called upon to open at the other end, he was similarly obliged to add a few paces to his run and really let fly. What followed was one of the most torrid opening spells I have witnessed at close hand — the bowling was very fast and furious — the batsmen were incidental, the two bowlers were displaying their feathers like bantam cocks. The tempo did not lessen and after a couple of overs, Mike struck first. The batsman's stumps went cartwheeling all over the place and Andy immediately congratulated the bowler saying "He was certainly fooled by your slower ball!" It virtually meant that the other aspiring bowlers in our side had to take second place — this was fast bowling almost at its best, and so difficult to contend with. Both our quickies subsequently played for the county.

Minor Counties Cricket — Time dims the memory and perhaps it is helpful at times to have accepted standards to allow comparisons to be made. North Devon is not a breeding ground for county cricketers (with one or two very notable exceptions), many of the grounds were rustic, and there were not many schools specialising in the sport. Probably for these reasons, county teams were usually made up of players from the more populated areas which in Devon would mean the east and south of the county. The main grounds were there, probably the weather was better, and travelling was much easier prior to the advent of motorways, trunk and link roads. In addition, Minor County matches were played over a two day period during the summer months and so schoolmasters were a fairly obvious choice both as regards availability during the school holidays and having played to a good standard at school/college.

I did mention earlier that I had been involved in a number of trial matches in 1953, the last of which was on a very wet wicket at Tiverton when our opening bowler ran through the opposition and JEC did not

"The batsman's stumps went cartwheeling all over the place . . ."

turn his arm. We said our goodbyes and in 1964 I was contacted and asked to play a two day friendly against The Royal Navy at Mount Wise, Plymouth. The good thing was I knew three of the other players quite well but, otherwise, I was in very strange territory, particularly having served as a gunner in the Royal Artillery! The whole event turned out to be a most enjoyable exercise, something not to be forgotten.

Another thing I shall never forget is that whilst I was able to motor the sixty miles to Plymouth for the game, public transport linking North Devon to this southern outpost was infrequent to say the least and certainly not direct. Grandad was not going to miss his grandson's debut for the county and somehow, in his seventies, he made it to the ground in time. I do not know to this day how he got there and now there is no chance of finding out.

I am not sure if I adopted the right attitude in that I had taken wickets regularly in friendly club cricket matches over a great number of years and now in my early thirties, ten years after the initial trials, I was being asked to play against the Royal Navy. I regarded this as "fodder" for the RN batsmen to give them a bit of confidence in a not too important game, and then for me to creep back up north to obscurity once more.

The first day went quite well with David Shepherd "crashing" sixty-three runs in quick time (this was a necessary tactic to get a result in four innings to be played in two days) and by the end of the day I had picked up two wickets, largely as a result of excellent catching. I was half-way through my ordeal, one day to go.

We were accommodated at "HMS *Drake*" in rather more luxury than we perhaps were used to at home and that evening drank in the officers' mess at the cricket ground. A number of the lads went off for a Chinese meal and we all met at the mess after ties (in some form or other!) had been found for one and all, this being a prerequisite for entry. My capacity for ale is small though I do enjoy a drink, and when we were joined by those who had eaten elsewhere, tongues became loose and we all had a very good time. Our captain was not with us, which probably was no bad thing, and amongst the banter, I was asked to expand on the idiosyncrasies of North Devon wickets and what I was trying to bowl!

I handed over my car keys to one of the senior members (there were no drink driving laws in those days but I thought this a prudent move) and quite a number of our players bundled into the car for the trip back to HMS *Drake*. After about five minutes, the substitute driver was able to get the windscreen wipers to work (it wasn't raining at the time!) as he was unfamiliar with that particular model of Vauxhall. We went back to HMS *Drake*, after identifying ourselves to those guarding HM's Navy, and slept very soundly indeed after the driver took a march past on the parade ground before saying good night to us all.

The officers' mess at HMS *Drake* is something else with an abundance of silverware, battle ensigns and petty officers waiting at tables, but we were adamant that this would not detract from the task in hand — the defeat of HM Navy.

After this splendid start to the day, we made our way to the ground and changed in readiness for a continuation of the Navy's first innings — they were chasing a total of one hundred and ninety-two. Our captain, a very strict disciplinarian, sidled up to me and said quietly, "Collins, I have heard all about what you intend to do to HM's Navy — you had better open the bowling but I do not want to see the double-arm swinger!." The nonsense conversations of the previous beer-ridden evening had found their way back to *"El capitaine"* via David Shepherd (I suspect), one of our senior players.

The game ended in an honourable draw and I had picked up five wickets in the two innings, far more preferable than just being "fodder". I had been very well received, felt that I had not let anyone down (particularly Grandad) but it was sad to hear (from

Devon's point of view) that David was being given a three year contract to play for Gloucestershire and that he would also be joined by our left-handed quick bowler, Jack Davey of Tavistock.

In fairness, Devon CCC had a very good side at that time and as an off-spinner, I was in competition with the captain, a brilliant player and all-seeing captain, and someone who, although a teacher from a Northern background, played for Devon and subsequently went on to play first-class cricket as a professional with two of the country's leading counties. In this context, perhaps I was very fortunate and from time to time had an airing with a very good team indeed, always being accepted and welcomed as one of the gang. I found parallels with my home club in that there were always some very intelligent players, and, deep down, they were playing for fun and the love of the game. As such, there was always time for a bit of nonsense.

The following year, I played at Exeter against Oxfordshire. I had never really seen a wicket like it — it was dark brown, almost black, and shiny. The match was not played to a full conclusion, one of the visitors scoring a hundred, and I remember having a drink that evening with one of the opposition, a delightful man who had represented the Minor Counties as a spin bowler against international touring sides, and he insisted on buying a drink for his "non-turning off-spinner friend". It was that hard. He did no better, and we won by way of outscoring our opponents on the first innings.

Doug Yeabsley, star bowler and useful batsman, was the county equivalent to 'Awke — they had much in common. Left hand quick bowlers, right hand batsmen, fine rugby players, both great leg pullers, and both respected teachers. Doug was already a legend on the Minor Counties circuit and known to most players so that it was not uncommon for him to dash off after a game to enjoy the evening and a jug or two with one of the opposition. After our fruitless day in the field, Doug was joined that evening by the opposition's opening fast bowler and together they went to a night club, I believe, in Dawlish. It had proved to be a very poor choice, totally lifeless, not much entertainment, and the beer was flat! They were thrown out.

I asked why. Being ready to leave, the Oxford quickie asked Doug in a very loud voice which echoed throughout the establishment "Doug, do you know why Hitler sacked his chambermaid?"

"I don't know, Tichers — why did Hitler sack his chambermaid?"

"Because she kept taking the piss out of the jerries!"

Both left the establishment rather hurriedly, with the help of staff, to resume hostilities on the cricket field the following day.

There were two other games I remember with affection. Devon won their way through to The Gillette Cup and quite obviously the one day game was much different to the normal Minor Counties two day outing, particularly when it came to playing against the first-class counties. I was well aware that by this time, my career at this level was not going to be a very long one due to my age, so the best thing I could do would be to savour the moment.

As preparation for the Gillette, Devon managed to arrange a match with Somerset CCC on the County Ground at Taunton. Here was the ground that I had visited regularly in my early teens as a spectator. I had idolised the players from the wooden seats around the ground, and I had looked towards the old wooden pavilion in awe of the great men who had emerged from that building to entrance the crowds packed into this intimate ground. Simply to go in through the wrought iron gates carrying a cricket bag was something else. It was not too serious a game in that it was a warm up for both our teams but in the context of the coming season, it was so important.

I remember little about that part of the game which we did play other than Somerset batted and rain stopped play in mid-afternoon. I could say, however, that I had played against Somerset CCC and on the

County Ground. My lasting memory was being asked to bowl against Greg Chappell. Acknowledged as one of the great Australian batsmen, I tried to work out some sort of plan. I had never seen such a high backlift and this was followed by immaculate timing and footwork. I got one past him once but this was not to be repeated and perhaps it is fair to say, I was saved by rain, though Somerset had only scored one hundred and sixty-nine for the loss if four wickets in fifty-two overs.

In 1968, I was privileged to play in a game which made a truly lasting impression and was something I shall remember for ever. A late burst of good results in the Minor Counties Championship left Devon in the unexpected position of needing a win against Cornwall away in the last game of the season, to possibly become second on points average in which case Devon could then challenge the undisputed leaders, Yorkshire II, for the championship. I was called in at the last minute as our star spinner was unavailable.

The game was played at Truro and the players gathered from various parts of the county and whilst I had a relatively unscathed drive down the north coast, the lads from the southern part of the county were obliged to go across the Tamar Bridge. It was not unusual for Doug Yeabsley and Gerald Trump to motor together with the ritual that as soon as they went across the bridge and reached the Cornish side, they would stop the car immediately, whatever the state of the traffic, then get out and kiss the pavement — they were in the land of "The rabbits" — or so they believed. Needless to say both were bowlers!

I was still very much a fringe player, perhaps not quite "fodder" when it came to such an important game, but the other ten had brought the team to this final elevated position. I walked into the changing room wearing a Groucho Marx mask, i.e. a rather big nose, glasses, heavy eyebrows and moustache, which my son had been given the previous Christmas. This immediately took the fancy of Doug.

The captain had obviously given great thought to his tactics for this so important game where it was almost essential for us to bat first, get a good score, and take a few wickets before the end of play on the first day, putting the opposition on the back foot immediately. And so it turned out to be. Devon won the toss and the captain elevated Doug from No.9 to open the innings. Doug was a very capable bat, but more often than not languished in the lower reaches to conserve his energy for his fast bowling. In his haste to pad up, he dropped his jockstrap onto the wooden floor and, having retrieved it, put it on without first checking for splinters — a fatal move. He suddenly realised that the edge of his bat was missing which gave him a narrowed weapon with which to defend himself and also score runs. He promptly got over this by asking if anyone had a red pen with which he drew a bull's-eye in the middle of his bat. Finally, he did not wish to give the Cornish opposition the opinion that he was an elevated No.9, and so asked if he could borrow the "Groucho Marx" mask, put it on, and away he went. He took his guard still wearing the mask, keeping as straight a face as possible, and when he had adequately made his mark at the crease to confirm his guard, he walked down the pitch to the Cornwall opening bowler and asked him to bowl for the bull's-eye he had drawn on his bat earlier. Doug and the Cornwall quickie were, of course, good friends of many years' standing, but what a start to what was to be a crucial and dramatic game.

The umpire did not flinch and seemed to regard the whole episode as a normal part of the game! Doug scored sixty-one runs, fully justifying his captain's decision to allow him to open the batting but not before several stoppages to remove splinters! Fair to say, it was a painful innings, but as Doug was always saying, "there is no gain without pain".

Chris Greetham, our former Somerset CCC batsman, did exactly what was asked of him by scoring a masterly eighty-four not out allowing Devon to declare at two hundred and fifty for five at tea. Everything was going

"I walked into the changing room wearing a Groucho Marx mask . . ."

to plan (except for the splinters). Cornwall ended the day at one hundred and four runs for the loss of five wickets.

That evening, we were rather confined to barracks at a small country hotel. This was perhaps understandable as the following day we would have to bowl out Cornwall quickly, score some very rapid runs ourselves and then bowl Cornwall out again, albeit on a wearing wicket. I remember sharing a room with Max Lloyd, a player from North Devon CC and very experienced having been capped as an opening batsman by both Devon and Wiltshire at Minor Counties level. Cornwall's star all-rounder had just come to the wicket prior to the close of play, and we all knew that if we took a few quick wickets early the following morning, we would be well on our way. Max, who was familiar with the majority of players on the Minor Counties circuit, was a mine of information and I thought he might help me by giving me some idea of the weaknesses of the batsmen to come so that I might go onto the field with a cunning plan. This was not to be and, in particular, he pretended to know little about the talented all-rounder. Max probably knew that if we played at our best, we would win.

Next morning, we were all up for it and as we walked out to the wicket, the captain asked me to carry on the good work (I had taken three wickets the previous evening). There facing me was the Cornish all-rounder, a good player well experienced in Minor County affairs, and my roommate had not been able to shed any light on his weaknesses. He oozed confidence.

We set an attacking field and from four paces, I launched the first missile of the day at the all-rounder. The first ball of the day, in a crucial Minor Counties match, and it turned out to be a full toss! I did not consider this to be in my normal armoury but the all-rounder was equally surprised and though he hit it forcibly, it was straight back at me. The ball shot through my hands, lodged in my midriff and it stayed there as I crouched to absorb the pain! I was able to hold that position long enough for the umpire to give the batsman out. The captain then came up and said "Well done, Collins, but for God's sake, use your hands next time!"

I was taken off shortly afterwards, Cornwall were all out for one hundred and fifty-nine runs and Devon threw bat at ball declaring at ninety-eight for the loss of four wickets, setting up a grand finale.

Thereafter the match went our way — brilliant catches were held, wickets fell just at the right time, and, with an hour to spare, Cornwall were back in the hutch for ninety-five all out. We had done enough to be runners-up with the prospect of a challenge against Yorkshire II, but this was a non-starter on account of cost, particularly at such a late stage in the season.

This was to be my final game in the Minor Counties and I was delighted to have taken eight wickets for sixty-six runs in the match, despite not having been a first choice bowler. Grandad was so pleased!

When things are going like this, cricket can seem quite an easy game, and with Cornwall on the back foot, I did not risk the "double arm swinger" but the Cornish quickie did get the "Miller roundarm". A left hand bat, I changed to around the wicket, bowling on or about the off-stump with the ball moving away. Having bowled four such deliveries, I threw in the "Miller roundarm", delivered from the edge of the crease, with a low arm quick delivery, and the ball whizzed past the batsman at a considerable speed, took the edge and was gobbled up. His comment as he passed me was "Where the f......hell did that come from!" I felt very indebted to Keith Miller.

The elation from taking part in such a game caused me to give considerable thought as to whether I ever wanted to play again. There could never be a more dramatic match, I could never play with a finer bunch of good cricketers who took me in as one of their own, although I had played little part in their exceptionally successful campaign. Perhaps the most rewarding thing about playing in this match was that I qualified to wear a county sweater. This required five Minor County appearances, unlike the present day when one appearance at any level permits the wearing of the county colours and insignia. In my opinion, the county sweater is to be worn with the greatest of pride and when wearing it, I feel that I should perform to an expected standard at least indicating that "I had done a bit". This is not easy when one is seventy!

And so, the final stage.

The Tourist — Tours took on a different persona. It was usual to go beyond one's own club and recruit a few "good" tourists, people who could add a bit of steel to the middle of the team, be it as regards batting or bowling. Then there would be good tourists in their own right — jolly good company and good for a beer or three! The club's playing reputation was not at stake but it was still important to win.

I met some wonderful people in both categories. Our club at one time organised a couple of short tours and we were able to hold our own with a good representative side but in general we were not into touring. One particular tour took us to Newbury where we had a very good weekend. We were due to play two fixtures and I remember that on the Friday evening, after quite a long drive, the evening food in Newbury did not go down too well with me and I had tummy trouble which, in all honesty, I could not put down to the local brew.

The next morning, I trekked the streets of Newbury in an attempt to shake off the discomfort but this had little effect and I was quite glad to hold on to one of our players as I walked along. The captain said that we were not too good in the reserves department and that, if at all possible, he would like me to play. I felt like death! I did one or two laps of the ground and still felt quite groggy but was eventually pressed into performing.

The captain's forcefulness worked and by the end of the afternoon, I had taken eight wickets for eight runs, holding a catch in the deep to dismiss the ninth. Perhaps it was just as well that I was ill!

What we did not realise was that the side we were due to play the next day had sent along a spy. I gather a committee meeting followed and when we turned up for the Sunday game, we were told that it was not usual to play with a new ball (or anything with a ridge resembling a seam to assist the spinners) and we were given a piece of leather which had received many a pummelling. I had to be content with six for twenty-two, having difficulty in finding a firm base against which to fix my spinning finger! Another lasting memory was a sign on the wall of the wooden village hall in which we changed stating that there should be "No smoking while dancing"! Most of our members were from the Victor Sylvester School of Dancing and did not know what the notice meant.

My happiest touring memories came from an association with members of the Raleigh Cricket Club at Barnstaple, which eventually toured under the name of "The Glow-worms". We were always well received in the Cheltenham area, one or two good players from other clubs joined the Raleigh players, and a few supporters made up the party. I can find no positive record of what actually happened which is perhaps good as only the more stupid aspects of the tours come to the fore now and again. What I do remember, however, is that we invariably had a dinner on the Saturday evening prior to returning home after playing on Sunday and this dinner would be attended by representatives of all the teams forming the opposition on our tour. We had some fabulous nights. The tour party was an incredible mix and we never seemed quite out of our depth playing against some very good sides on a variety of pitches, most good, but there were exceptions and we had to contend with whatever changes were brought about by the September weather. Mostly this meant slightly damp pitches and hope for the spin bowler.

One of my first recollections was of Johnny Townes, a thin scruffy looking young man, who liked a pint or two but in addition had a tremendous sense of humour. He was always good fun to have about, never did anyone any harm, and I, for one, certainly enjoyed his company. It was suggested that he would consume about fifteen pints of lager during a lunch hour (maybe two) — I think this was an exaggeration, though I never counted. The outcome was that, by the time the match started, he was a little under the weather though it was sometimes difficult to tell. In addition, when in this state, he was emphatic that he could speak Morse code!

On one particular tour, I missed the first day and agreed to meet the team at its overnight venue the following morning, so that we could make our way together to Cheltenham. I enquired how the team had got on in the opening game.

"Splendidly" came the reply.

"And who got the runs?" I asked.

"Johnny" came the reply "but he was out as soon as he sobered up!" There may have been some truth in this.

The next day, however, as a reward, Johnny was invited to open once again. This time, the great 'Awke was standing as umpire and asked Johnny what guard he required. The preliminaries were duly carried out, the opening bowler tore up, sent down an extremely good ball scattering Johnny's stumps. Johnny looked up at 'Awke and politely said "I'm ready now!" Whether he was aware that a ball had actually been bowled, we shall never know, but 'Awke quickly had to assume the authority of the white coat and pointed to the pavilion.

The other slightly disconcerting thing that particular morning was that the police were in attendance at breakfast taking statements from some of our players. This was not to be expected and I asked my good friend and wicketkeeper Andy what was happening. It appeared that at this particular country hotel, there were regular floor shows, in fact some of the best acts in the country had appeared there from time to time. Amidst the acts the previous evening, there had been a young couple who did a dancing act which involved the removal of clothing.

"I'm ready now!"

At the end of the first half, the lady was on something resembling a cross with the young man taking off all her clothes to music and scattering the garments amongst the audience. The second half opened with the young man on the cross and the young lady doing a mirrored version of the earlier performance. Apparently at one time they had simply been dancers, opening and closing shows, but the demand for this had lessened whilst the more artistic presentation was much in demand. By the time the second half started, Johnny was well into his lager and announced quite loudly that if she took his boots off, he was going to leave! The remainder of his apparel was removed in a delightful manner (so I am told) to a musical accompaniment and almost the last garment to be removed (and projected into the audience as was the remainder of his dress) was his gold lamé jockstrap. This was hurled with great aplomb to a roll of the drums into the baying audience.

The curtains came down and a few minutes later, the duo appeared wrapped in bathrobes to collect their discarded apparel. The gold lamé jockstrap was not found! The matter was serious enough to report to the police, they could not attend until breakfast time to take statements, by which time the robbers could well have departed at speed, the motorway being close by.

Whilst most of the cricketers gave statements, which did nothing to assist in the detection of the missing apparel, we all held out breath waiting to see which of our members would be wearing a gold lamé jockstrap to the wicket that afternoon. No one obliged!

One season, I broke my middle finger playing against one of the sides we were visiting. It was a painful situation and I ended up with a large metal covering, bound on to ensure that the finger mended in an approximately straight position. Sadly, this was not to be and with a damaged middle index finger on the right hand, I suspect that some of my earlier spinning ability had diminished. For a while, if I was minded to join in the cricket, it was as an umpire and to give a batsman out, it was not just a question of raising one digit, but this was accompanied by the splinted middle finger, giving the impression of the "V" sign to the batsman, and, amongst friends, I felt obliged to advise them of this at the outset.

By the end of the season I had recovered reasonably well and went on tour again. One of the Barnstaple members asked how the finger was and I explained that I could no longer straighten the finger and had lost the feeling at one end. He was quick to tell me that there was a part of his body which suffered in exactly the same way!

I had always been told what a beautiful ground there was at Stinchcombe, a short distance from Cheltenham. International touring sides often played there and it was indeed an honour for us to make a visit. This was well into the tour and there were one or two sore heads about, in addition to which we heard that the home side had one or two very good players from the universities and Gloucester seconds.

The pitch was damp and the ball moved about quite a bit and at pace and, in truth, only one of our recognised batsmen, Nick Barrington, put up any resistance and he made half of our ninety runs. In addition, the innings did not last until tea time and the home side were able to begin the chase in late afternoon.

Our skipper for the day was a splendid cricketer, Percy Heritage, who had moved into the area with his employment. He was a particularly good leg-spinner and having regard to the wicket and our low score, he decided to open with two spinners. The batsmen were no fools and it was obviously going to be a considerable struggle against the county and varsity men and we knew that we would be pushed to bowl our opponents out. Nevertheless, we set about our task.

The ball was turning from the very off and it was certainly going to be uncomfortable for the batsmen, but we had to keep the pressure on. I believe an early wicket fell — we were on our way, but then we received a body blow. I bowled to the opener, he played slightly inside the line, and the ball whipped back to clip his off stump. I was bowling to my usual club keeper who always made a point of standing back smartly when this happened as an indication that he had played no part in the bail coming off. The batsman stood his ground. I was obliged to appeal and the umpire at my end said he could not see as the batsman had moved across his wicket. Our umpire at square leg was challenged — "Sorry, I was rolling a fag — I didn't see anything." There could only be one decision. We then took tea.

I saw the batsman and said to him "I bowled you out there just now."

"I know" he replied, "but I don't walk if you only hit one stump!"

Just after tea, I was able to ask the umpire if he was out when I hit all three, or perhaps he wasn't ready! Needless to say, we won.

One of our "bankers" on any tour was Nick Barrington, a truly amazing sportsman and winner. He would talk himself into a score in whatever situation, whilst looking particularly vulnerable with a loping gait and pebblestop glasses. I umpired one game against our hosts, Woodmancote CC, on this particular tour and, whilst we were not exactly in trouble, we needed runs on the board and they were not coming quite as quickly as we would have wished. A very mediocre bowler came on and immediately bowled Nick a short long hop. This was patted back to the bowler with the cry "Well bowled." A much better ball on the leg stump was flicked away for four — "So sorry, old man, the ball was much too good for me." Another long hop — "Well bowled." A flick around the corner and comment to the bowler "How unlucky can you get!" The captain was within hearing distance and the appraisal of the bowling performance by the batsman must have been pleasing to the ear but it was at the expense of eight runs an over. After six overs, the captain was obliged to reassess the situation. Nick had scored fifty and the bowler had not taken any wickets! By this time we were almost out of sight.

It was almost an inbuilt strategy whenever he was in competition. One morning we played golf. Nick played off a single figure handicap, looked ungainly when addressing the ball, but seemed to hit fair and true without much bother though his arm action probably meant that he would not unduly worry Tiger Woods. It is somewhat disarming when just as one is departing into the back swing, a voice is heard to say "You do get a stroke on this hole, old man, don't you?" In such a situation, the ball rarely goes in the right direction and a "Sorry, did I put you off?" isn't exactly a true recompense. The supplier of the golf balls, however, was absolutely delighted, he owned a supermarket and had his brand name plastered all over the balls which I had distributed throughout the length and breadth of the golf course.

During the afternoon, Nick scored his usual fifty runs and he took me aside to ask what I was doing that evening. "Nothing" I replied, and he asked me to say nothing about the fact that the locals had heard he was in town and wanted him to take on the county champion at squash. We did not want a drunken mob of cricketers baying him on and so it was — I was his sole supporter. He duly despatched the county champ but being an international player himself, perhaps one should expect that — golf, cricket, squash, they all came the same to this remarkable sportsman.

It is never much fun playing in the rain however much one would like to see a result. We were involved in the game when the rain started to come down very steadily. The home side which was batting made no attempt to curtail the activity — the ball was getting more and more slippery, sweaters were getting longer. In the end, Nick said in an extremely loud voice "The last time I played in the rain, one of the b....rs died of pneumonia." We were off in no time — he was a man of great presence and authority!

Whilst paying tribute to this remarkable man, one of

the national daily newspapers set up a competition to find the country's No.1 sportsman. I was able to paint a very good picture of Nick. Not only was he an international squash player and more than useful golfer, he also captained the Cornish Choughs at cricket, kept goal in the South Western Soccer League and played stand-off half for Falmouth at rugby football. Later he was to go on and play hockey for Truro.

Quite a number of sportsmen were able to excel at two or three sports, but Nick's talents knew no bounds. I duly sent off details of my nomination and received a call at the office thanking me for the nomination and asking if I would go to London the following day to discuss my nomination with the newspaper editor. This was almost too quick for comfort and I felt uneasy about something, prompting me to make further enquiries. The call had come from Nick's secretary! The national newspaper knew Nick as his brother was a world champion sportsman and, having been tipped off that some idiot had nominated him, Nick took it from there and decided to get his own back. The nomination was serious and I am sure Nick would have been in the running had he not decided to get his own back on his idiot friend.

Many of the participants on tour undertook the trip as a therapy and break from the normal routine, and it was often surprising to find who was in the touring party. Not all of us were able to get away for the beginning of the tour and on one particular occasion, two of us were to follow on the second day. We got in touch and I suggested that we might go in my car as I had a reasonable large boot which would take both cricket gear and golf clubs. "No, let's have lunch at Barnstaple, then we can make our way in my car — I have to take the boys back to school" came the reply. The argument went to and fro and finally I gave in and agreed to meet at an hotel, have lunch and share his car. My wife left me at the hotel with a pile of luggage, mostly indicative of a sporting weekend. My friend arrived, with wife and two boys, and we all enjoyed lunch, leaving my luggage in the foyer. It was then time to move on. I had many hands to assist me with my luggage and we made our way to ....a Rolls-Royce! I had never even ridden in one, let alone one with a personalised number plate. I had to concede that perhaps the boot was bigger than my Audi!

I was allowed to ride in front. We glided to Millfield School and bade farewell to the two boys. My "chauffeur" was (and is, up to the time of writing this book) a good friend for whom I have acted in a professional capacity, and he asked if I would like to see his new supermarket in the centre of the town, which had been established with the express idea of assisting in the paying of fees for the boys at the nearby school. We stopped on double yellows (you can do that sort of thing in a "Roller") and as we stepped out of the car, two attractive young ladies walked by and I was delighted to hear them say "I wonder which group they play for?" That did wonders for the ego, being taken as a rock star!

We had a spare morning and Brian asked if I was doing anything. I replied "No" and he suggested that I go with him without announcing the fact to the others. We headed for Worcester. It was not the most relaxing of drives as the fuel indicator started flashing at a time when garages were giving stamps depending on the volume of petrol purchased. Some garages offered three stamps per gallon, some four, and Brian insisted that with such a large tank, it would have to be four. The number of garages we passed, and I swear the light was getting brighter. I did not fancy pushing a "Roller"!

We subsequently refuelled, Brian told me we were looking for a certain factory, and I espied a large building in the distance which looked as if it might be our destination. We pulled into the managing director's slot (you can do this sort of thing with a Rolls) and a deputation immediately emerged from the factory to sort us out. Brian introduced himself, pointed to me suggesting that I was his financial advisor, and we were immediately decked out in white smock and hat in time for a tour of the factory.

What I did not know at the time was that Brian was looking to purchase a vast number of tins of baked beans for his supermarkets and to make sure he selected the best beans at the best price, he had various members of his staff "testing" beans purchased in other establishments and marking them up as regards taste, price, presentation, etc. After collating all the information which had been gathered, a final decision had been made based on results, and further enquiries suggested that the factory at Worcester was the producer, hence our visit.

We were ushered into the factory. The sacks of beans were loaded at one end; the bags were sliced open; the contents were disgorged onto an oscillating belt where attentive workers removed by hand the blackened and substandard beans, and thereafter the beans proceeded along a progressive route changing their substance from natural beans to baked beans in a tin, with appropriate label which could either be stuck on or painted on the tin. It was all mesmerising — brilliant in concept — but I would have hated working on the shop floor and having to look at beans all day long. Brian and I nodded to each other over the beans — this could be the answer.

On looking around a little more, however, we were able to see that many of the different types of beans which Brian's staff had been testing were all processed and canned in this very factory. In other words, you can go into the various supermarkets and buy branded goods, but it is not beyond the pale that in many cases the content is exactly the same, it is only the price and label which differ.

The morning ended with Brian looking across the table at me and saying "What do you think?"

"Very impressive."

We signed a contract for two hundred and fifty thousand tins of baked beans, Brian signing first and sliding the contract across to me for my signature. I must say, I liked being in the big time!

It was rather nice to get back to the rest of the team

who were quick to ask what we had been doing that morning. It isn't often that you get the chance to say "We bought two hundred and fifty thousand tins of baked beans!"

There was the time when one of our new tourists put in for an early call and the call came before he had gone to bed! Apparently this is not uncommon.

Frampton on Severn was the scene of one of the most peculiar matches I have ever taken part in. The weather in the west can be uncertain in September and this particular year was no exception. The better grounds might not be risked with a late game against tourists and the Saturday game was due to be played at a works ground which, at quite a late stage, was declared too wet to play on. Our Cheltenham hosts, however, were anxious to fit us up with some kind of game and after many frantic telephone calls, we were told that Frampton would host us despite the fact that officially they had played their last game of the season a few weeks ago. When you go on tour, it is with a view to playing cricket and so we were very obliged to Frampton for giving us a go.

We changed in something resembling a village cinema with folding seats on each side and a pair of emergency fire doors opened onto what looked more like a soccer pitch than a cricket field. Along the boundaries, there were four flags in total, one in each corner! On the opposite side of the ground to the cinema was a road along which passed rather large red buses — at very regular intervals. Apologies were made for the fact that the club had played its last official game two weeks ago and that last week, there had been a village fair and fete in that very field. This accounted for the bottle tops and straws, some of which had unfortunately been rolled (with a heavy roller) into the wicket.

They were a pleasant crowd and who were we to grumble — they had made a very special effort to provide us with a game of cricket.

The home team batted first and initially the tourist bowlers had difficulty in contending with the elements.

The quickie (not very quick by this time as we were nearing the end of the tour) found that his normal delivery was greatly wind-assisted by something approaching a force seven gale off the River Severn and so there was a liberal sprinkling of full tosses which did not seek assistance from the pitch. At the other end, the opening bowler ploughed into the wind and at times looked as if he was running backwards, but his supreme stamina enabled him to complete one over.

Our captain had to quickly review the situation and decided to let one of the slower bowlers tackle the gale head on and the quickies would share the other end. The batsmen, meanwhile, were deciding upon their own policy and with the introduction of spin, one of the batsmen quickly established supremacy by suggesting that his co-opener was much better at playing spin than he was (he had seen the ball turning!), and he should endeavour to stay at the Severn end, and the master opener would face the gale and the quick bowler, hoping to take advantage of the full tosses and in the knowledge that the leg side boundary was very close at hand.

I was to field at square leg which, in fact, was actually on the boundary itself. This seemed extremely close to the wicket and to satisfy my own curiosity, I paced out the distance between wicket and boundary and found it to be twenty-two paces off the square, about the same length as a cricket pitch. This in itself was the same for both sides (though they did not have a batsman of the calibre of Andy!) but it was somewhat disconcerting when a batsman struck out lustily towards the boundary and as one was swooping down to field a ball, a No.5 red bus went by within earshot! As the afternoon wore on, it was apparent that the No.5 was a very regular service indeed.

Not only did the ball turn amidst the bottle tops and straws, but by angling the seam away from the batsman and letting the ball flow into the gale, a boomerang effect was created. Whilst the batsmen at the Severn end struggled manfully, the crafty opener at the other end gave continuous verbal encouragement to the incoming batsmen who, by this time, were changing at quite regular intervals, the ball spinning and swinging appreciably.

Eventually Nos.9 and 10 arrived at the wicket and departed off successive balls which gave rise to something of a dilemma. There was no No.11! The home captain enquired as to whether we would like him to go into the football match next door and find someone to bat at No.11 so that I could attempt the hat trick. This seemed a very generous gesture which my captain and I gave very serious consideration, but we declined. It was not really fair to tear someone away from his soccer match just to be made a fool of and, in any case, he might not get out. Perhaps it was far better to go through the entire winter in the knowledge that I had a hat trick on and that the first ball of the next season would be something to really look forward to.

This had happened to Bill Shortridge some years before when he took two wickets with his last two balls of the season, but sadly he had a heart attack during the winter. 'Awke was very quick to comment that this was not unexpected having regard to the fact that Bill had to go through the whole winter with the thought of a possible hat trick on his mind — enough to break any man!

To get back to the match at Frampton, the home side eventually mustered one hundred and twenty runs on that windswept afternoon and this may have seemed a fairly respectable total having regard to the conditions, but captain Andy had been gazing at the twenty-two yard boundary all afternoon. He was a great leg-side player and could sweep most bowlers with ease wherever the ball pitched. Andy opened, we knocked off the runs easily with Andy scoring eighty not out, mostly leg-side boundaries. In fairness, we were very thankful to Frampton for making a very special effort to put on a match for us that afternoon, which we all enjoyed to the full.

Whilst extolling Andy's prowess on the leg side, we

went to Tiverton for a league match, and the game was progressing quite nicely on a splendid summer's afternoon. Andy went in, quickly settled and a good medium paced bowler pitched a ball just outside the off stump which Andy hooked around the corner for four. The bowler did not appreciate such treatment, commented aloud that he thought it was a lucky shot and Andy, always composed at the wicket, suggested to the gentleman that he should pitch the next one in the same place. He duly obliged, and the ball found its way into the top of a tree well over a lengthy boundary! It was no fluke, just Andy playing to his strengths and many a bowler (including myself) have had exactly the same treatment so the best thing is to try and pitch the ball elsewhere.

There are quite a number of local batsmen in this category and it certainly is no use feeding them, but rather, as a slow bowler, one should concentrate on weaknesses rather than strengths though it sometimes takes a while to learn this lesson and it can be painful.

I do enjoy a good after dinner speaker. They vary considerably as regards delivery and approach, but you were always in for a good evening when the local doctor, the well-known "Leader" (referred to in the fishing episode) was on the toast list. In retrospect, many of his "true" stories would now rank as sexist or racist but they were, nevertheless, very funny at the time and whilst not to be repeated in public, often raise a smile when they "pass across the inward eye".

After making his mark as a local speaker, "The Leader" had his first book published. It was not the first he had written, and there had been many rejections, but once a book had found favour, his earlier works were unearthed and revitalised, and his publishers looked at many of these in a new light. This new modicum of fame as an author brought with it some benefits which included radio interviews, book signings and, on one occasion, he was even asked to judge a "beauty competition".

This was completely unknown ground and so he

asked a friend for some advice and it was suggested that "The Leader" should ask the young ladies their name, vital statistics, and what they did for a living. This would be a good start and, hopefully, he could take it from there. One had the feeling that with this and other adventures in life, "The Leader" was looking for a story that he could amplify to advantage and this proved no exception.

Came the evening, "The Leader" felt reasonably confident, and was introduced to the audience. The first young lady came on, a lovely looking girl with blonde hair, and "The Leader" asked "What is your name?"

"Andrea" came the reply.

"And what are your measurements?"

"36, 24, 35."

"And what do you do?"

"I would like to be a missionary in darkest Africa and help save the children there." This drew great applause.

The second girl came on, a brunette. She was Magda, 38, 25, 37, and her ambition was to improve the lot of those who lived in the rainforests of Brazil, were strangers to civilisation and only by hunting daily managed to remain alive.

The third was not quite in the same mould, she was considerably larger, but notable for her mass of curly, jet black hair. "And what is your name?"

"Big Julie" came the firm reply.

"And what are your measurements?"

"54, 38, 50."

"And what do you do?"

"Keep falling over!"

What is this to do with a book on cricket, I hear you ask? "The Leader" could certainly tell a good tale.

It was one Sunday morning in September. We had enjoyed good hospitality in Cheltenham — too good really — it even included a visit to a brewery where we were invited to sample the specimens retained from individual vats in case there were any complaints from outlets supplied from those vats when the original could be analysed and any justifiable complaints could be dealt with. Kept in ideal conditions, the specimens were probably looked after much better than the alehouse version but at some stage, the specimens had to be disposed of and it was perhaps fortuitous that we were on hand to assist in the disposal.

Driving down the main road from Cheltenham towards Bristol had to be a very steady jaunt that morning and, as we were due to perform at Flax Bourton that afternoon, we decided to leave the main road and find a quiet hostelry to sit and chill out. We turned off at Severn Beaches and found such an establishment, obviously well patronised having regard to the number of vehicles parked outside. We wended our way towards the entrance and were greeted at the door by someone who declared "You're just in time for Big Julie." I could not believe my ears! "The Leader" had been prone to exaggeration at times and we had taken his excellent yarn with the pinch of salt it deserved, but here was a version of "Big Julie". When she eventually appeared, she did have a wonderful head of curly black hair, and she was large! I mean large, large!

We had to pay an admittance fee (our umpire protested at this, but he was sixty) and sat down to watch what was a very usual Sunday lunch-time strip show as would appear to have been the norm in and around Bristol at that time. The early performers looked like skinny housewives out to earn a quick "bob". They were pale, not very coordinated and the harder they tried, the worse it became, but, after all, we were there for the beer and "Big Julie".

"Big Julie" eventually came on. She was not particularly well dressed (neither quantity or quality) and her undulations were certainly not in time with the background music which was being played. Her one prop was a banana which she waved around dramatically but it could not be seen to have any practical use. By the time the music stopped, she had forgotten to take her clothes off, the banana was "virgo intacto" and she brought the house down! I still do not know to this day what her attraction was but her great asset was knowing how to hold an audience, and, in fairness, she did not fall over once! I was delighted to have met THE Big Julie and only wish "The Leader" had been with me at that time.

Finale — The years rolled on and continue to roll, but perhaps without the "magic" that went before. Had I played later, I should not have known some of the splendid characters who crossed my path in the early days, yet I have no doubt that I should have enjoyed playing, though, I am sure, not to the same degree. The body now grows old, the ball does not turn as much, the "Miller roundarm" is no more, as with pace and movement lacking, it is little more than a gentle long-top on the leg side to be struck as far as the batsman would wish. I can still gaze at the pitch and the memories flood back, in addition to which a morning's shopping in nearby Barnstaple will produce at least one "hello" from someone with whom I have jousted over twenty-two yards in the past.

Let us leave it there — a glorious time, happily remembered by all as a time when sportsmanship was an honoured word, challenged only on the rarest of occasions.

Finally, I have done my best to recall events relying upon newspaper reports, Grandad's scrapbook and an ailing memory. Others may recall some of the events referred to in a slightly different light but I have done my best to convey a time when the game tolerated characters, we had fun, and gave enjoyment to many. I hope no one will take offence at my genuine attempt to document the period if only from a biased Bideford CC point of view.

The words of John Fry of Braunton perhaps say it all. The worst form of sledging during his long and illustrious career came when he approached the wicket in a somewhat lost cause for Braunton against Bideford and was greeted by 'Awke with the words "Cometh the hour, cometh the man". That meant so much to them both and hopefully sums up the feelings of the author.

Bideford Grammar School 1st XI, 1948. Back, Tony Grant, C. T. (Chic) Mill, Tony Down, Brian Rogers, Michael Goss, Peter Adams, D. (Motto) Mounce, Des Bennett. Front, Peter Loughlin, Rodney Beer, C. W. Stephenson, H. Oiseau Bird, 'Bandy' Walker, Philip Fulford, Tony Bond.

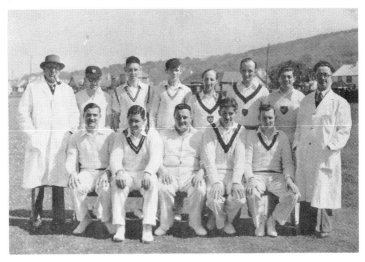

Bideford CC, 1953. Back. Capt H. V. Cope, R. (Ramadin) Mills, Peter Adams, Joe Pilling, Tony Baylis, Cliff Cudmore, Peter Williams, Jack Sinclair. Front. Alan Bidgood, Geoff Hawke, Ray Bird (Capt), Roy Parsons, Gerry Waldon.